COMMENDATION FOR DR. PRESTON WILLIAMS II's BOOK

Acclaimed leaders, pastors, and CEOs have
written endorsements saying:

"Dogmatics are timely, but principles are everlasting"; so said my Seminary Professor. He, along with Dr. Williams, have unparalleled precedent from the greatest teacher that ever lived! The gospels are filled with the parables (principles) that Jesus used to explain the Kingdom of God. Dr. Williams has written a riveting example of that genre. It will stimulate your thinking, and all who read it will be improved and empowered by his gifted applications!

Dr. Charles Travis
President and Founder, Logos Global Network
Chancellor, Logos University
Jacksonville, Florida

The God of How *is enjoyable reading. The stories, the life experiences, and the biblical principles are truly an exposition of purpose and DESTINY. It challenges us to remember that destiny is not where you end up, but the necessary succession of events that takes place in your life that will make you into the man or woman that God created you to be. Hey folks, especially Chapter 6! Check it out and pay attention; there you'll find the secret to fulfilling your purpose and destiny. To the author—my friend, Dr. Preston Williams II, a job well done.*

Bishop Wayne Babb
Founding Bishop and President of Oasis Church International
CEO, Community Development Corporation
Author of *Pillars: Building to Last*
Phenix City, Alabama

Facing the challenge of understanding life and how to respond to the many challenges, changes, temptations and opportunities that are a part of life is every man's struggle.

In this book, Dr. Williams shares the triumphs and the trials in such a way that we can all relate. There is tremendous encouragement in knowing that "you are not alone" as you face God's preparation for purpose. The stories shared here makes the important point that life is a process which never ends and even though we do not always understand, especially when some of those experiences are painful, God is with us. The very sobering principle of suffering and unexpected challenges to Kingdom citizens is clearly indicated and is certainly a necessary truth.

This book will challenge you, encourage you, and motivate you to continue to trust when you don't understand or see the bigger picture. The fact that Dr. Williams has bared himself in this book adds to its authenticity and personal value for every person. This is a must read and I highly recommend it to you.

Dr. Richard Pinder
Pastor/Sr. Vice President
Bahamas Faith Ministries International
Trustee, International Third World Leaders Association
Presbyter, International Fellowship of Ministers
Author of *Work: Your Signature*
Nassau, Bahamas

The God of How *is stimulating. It garnered my undivided attention and provoked soul searching. The stories were as if someone were peering into the portal of my thoughts and life. They incited a resurgence of memories long forgotten. The truths learned justly captured the essence of understanding how trials, transitions, and triumphs fit into God's plan for our life.*

Each of life's experiences has left an indelible imprint in our memory as a memorial of divine purpose and process; thus, inspiring us to be bridge builders for those who follow. The author's transparency is astonishing; the principles are profound, as well as, genuinely thought-provoking. To the author, my friend, and my brother, you have done an outstanding job!

Rev. Dr. Gwendolyn W. Mungin
Associate Minister
Church of God Sanctuary of Praise
Jacksonville, Florida
City Manager—Kingsland, Georgia
(2004-2013)

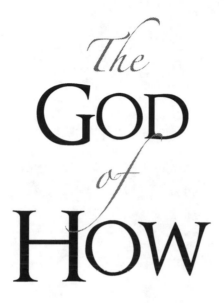

The
GOD
of
HOW

*Understanding How Trials, Transitions, and
Triumphs Fit into God's Plan for Your Life*

DR. PRESTON WILLIAMS II

Author of *Necessary Changes*

THE GOD OF HOW
UNDERSTANDING HOW TRIALS, TRANSITIONS, AND TRIUMPHS FIT INTO GOD'S PLAN FOR YOUR LIFE

iUniverse books may be ordered through booksellers or by contacting:

iUniverse
1663 Liberty Drive
Bloomington, IN 47403
www.iuniverse.com
1-800-Authors (1-800-288-4677)

Because of the dynamic nature of the Internet, any web addresses or links contained in this book may have changed since publication and may no longer be valid. The views expressed in this work are solely those of the author and do not necessarily reflect the views of the publisher, and the publisher hereby disclaims any responsibility for them.

Scripture quotations marked NKJV are taken from the New King James Version. Copyright © 1982 by Thomas Nelson, Inc. Used by permission. All rights reserved.

Any people depicted in stock imagery provided by Thinkstock are models, and such images are being used for illustrative purposes only. Certain stock imagery © Thinkstock.

ISBN: 978-1-4917-1120-0 (sc)
ISBN: 978-1-4917-1122-4 (hc)
ISBN: 978-1-4917-1121-7 (e)

Library of Congress Control Number: 2013918770

Print information available on the last page.

iUniverse rev. date: 06/20/2017

Dedication

I WOULD LIKE TO dedicate this book to Mrs. Pearl Brown-Williams (1926-2000) and Bishop Preston Williams Sr. (1928-2007) who departed this world to be with the Lord. Parents who made sure their children were raised knowing and loving God and whose presence is felt among us still.

Your foundation of faith and perseverance is instilled within me. You gave me the moral tools to support the discovery and use of my gifts. Those tools serves as the catalyst that drives me to give my very best in ministry.

And to all of my loving family, with boundless gratitude, who in their love and kindness have been a significant influence and inspiration in my life. I love you dearly.

Table of Contents

This is the very perfection of man, to find out his own imperfection
~ Saint Augustine

Preface

OF MY PREVIOUS BOOKS, this is the first of its kind in the way it captures personal stories of pivotal moments in my life and my teachings on the topic of life transitions in print. This manuscript is the sequel to my previous book *Necessary Changes*. In *Necessary Changes*, like *The God of How*, they didn't just happen. From several years of lectures, seminars, and sermons, they grew slowly. From tender roots planted in well-prepared soil, *The God of How* sprouted, leafed, budded, and blossomed. It has been a very special project brought into fruition through observations, research, and personal experiences. It is a reflection of stories from my past and the principles I have learned along the way. It is what has happened to all of us at some point in our lives.

The God of How is a summation of maturing ideas garnered from thirty plus years of service in the people business. It is a collaboration of the trials and joys I experienced. It is a work birthed not only from the solitary moments of a writer's retreat, but rather, in the midst of living. It is a collection of thoughts that I've pondered, researched, and studied. The principles I will share with you are influenced by great thinkers and mentors I've admired. The ideas gradually emerged into illuminating principles that turned into convictions.

I have dedicated my adult life striving to help people become their very best *selves*—to gain the confidence and inner freedom derived from the struggles of life. We face lifelong challenges, and the struggle to conquer them is difficult. I can identify with your struggles in the arena of life, but I understand and accept that my struggles are necessary for my strides, and my setbacks are actually setups for the greater blessings that are apportioned to my life's journey.

As a minister, I am committed to mastering the art of living. I am passionate about experiencing life the way God intended for it to be lived. A famous quote of William Wordsworth was paraphrased as saying, "art is passion recollected in tranquility." I don't believe that I have reached the tranquil part of the art of life's journey yet. Nevertheless, I no longer feel overwhelmed by my transitions. I can reflect on them, hold them at arm's length and consider anew what transitions really are and what they do to a person.

As a motivational speaker, my transitions earned me dividends as they helped me to better understand life and positioned me to motivate others. I have read many books about life and its countless issues. I have lectured, ministered, and counseled on just about every aspect of interpersonal relationships. So as I began this manuscript, I wanted to compose a book that would be different from others on the topic of life and the changes that are necessary to having a winning attitude toward life. It needed to be a book that placed life experiences into simple, practical context. In my opinion, once something is understood, a current of peace is released. This current of peace opens up our minds and hearts for meaningful actions which will ultimately lead to progress at its best and good success.

Simply put, *The God of How* is about understanding life's trials, transitions, and triumphs to help better manage how we respond to them. It is a book of understanding why you are going through what you're going through at this time in your life. It is about your relationship with yourself, your friends, your loved ones, and the choices you must make at different points during your journey toward becoming the best you there can be. It is about changing those things in your life that can be changed and accepting those you cannot change, and trusting God with His plans and purposes.

Throughout this book, you will be thoroughly introduced to the major theme of *The God of How*, called the circles of experiences with the cycles of life—trials, transitions, and triumphs. I strongly urge you to read with an open mind and a changeable heart as I take you on a personal journey of discovery of self and God's participation in the affairs of mankind.

Acknowledgments

FOR GIVING ME LIFE so that God can fulfill His purpose apportioned to me, I want to thank my parents. To my late father, Bishop Preston Williams Sr., although our relationship had its bumps and struggles in my early years, thank you for our reconciliation in the later years and our time together. They were precious. To my late mother, Pearl Brown Williams, you were such an awesome mother to me. Thank you for your laughter and your smiles and for providing the love and nurture that was critical for my development from a boy to a man.

I want to thank my lovely wife, Kathy, whose belief in this book's value to the precious body of Christ (and those who will later come to know Him) have spurred me through the challenges of spinal surgery and recovery in the midst of completing this manuscript. Thank you for putting up with the many late nights and awkward schedules so that the work could be accomplished. Your helpful editorial suggestions and encouragement have been a great blessing to me and I trust to others as well. Yours was the understanding and encouragement I greatly needed. I love you immeasurably.

I would also like to recognize my Senior Pastor and First Lady of Evangel Assembly Church in Temple Hills, MD, the Rev. Dr. St. Clair Mitchell and First Lady Judith Mitchell for their passionate leadership and spiritual covering. Thank you for your thought provoking life changing sermons, and your tenacity and sensitivity to

God's vision and ultimate plan for the Evangel Assembly Church. It was one of your sermons you preached a few years ago that inspired me to title this book, "The God of How." It is a privilege for Kathy and me to have you both as pastor and friend. Thank you for your service in the Kingdom of God.

I, along with Kathy, feel a deep sense of gratitude to our children and their families: Preston III, Jarell Sr., Portia, Sharmayne, and Zaynah. Your love, patience, and zest for life and pursuing your dreams is an inspiration. Don't ever give up! As I watch you face the challenges in your personal lives, I am encouraged to continue in developing and serving my gifting to the world.

Thanks especially to my editor, Maryanne Manning, for her delicate handling of the content of this manuscript—reviewing and critiquing each chapter with meticulous precision. Maryanne's editorial and conceptual expertise make her not only the best editor, but the nicest as well.

To the reader, the fact that you've chosen this literature for your personal library says that you are a visionary who has the desire and the courage to change. Thanks for making this choice.

Finally, to the source of all we can ask or think, the God of *how*, the Father and Lord of all creation, and His Son, Jesus Christ, and my personal Counselor, the Holy Spirit. Thank you for the privilege of knowing and serving You.

Prologue

THE CALL TO MINISTRY came during my teenage years, but I was a reluctant soul. I never saw myself doing what my father did as a profession. Some would say that it was the last thing on the list of career paths. I would say that becoming a minister was never on my list. It wasn't until I was an adult that I accepted the call of God upon my life. I was twenty-one years old. As foolish as this may sound, I gave in to the call of God with conditions—yeah right?! As if I was in a position to question or condition Him. My condition was simple, I just wanted to "do" ministry differently. I knew there was another level of ministry than what I had become accustomed to as a young man born and raised in a religious home in the 60s and 70s; little did I know He would grant my request. But what I didn't know is that it would come at a price, one that I, at that time, could never imagine.

The God of How is a transparent look into excerpts from my life's journey that help me to *become*. It is a book of process. I wanted to make this a book of not only important lifestyle principles, but also to bring to life and add context to these principles by including a few of my own personal life experiences in the form of short stories. The stories are not meant to be my personal memoir, but rather carefully selected pivotal and defining moments in my evolving understanding of God and His process in my life cycle of development—which is the premise of my inspiration to write this book.

Unfortunately, for the purpose of discretion and privacy, except for names and places and certain disguised details, the stories are true. Examples like those found throughout the book lend themselves to generalizations. Still, for many of us, parts of the stories will strike uncomfortably close to home. With the proper mental filters in place, appropriating the process of God to an experience is both psychologically and spiritually important. It is imperative to maintaining a biblical faithful, exemplary witness. I call it "developmental transparency."

Most individuals do not have the privilege of retreating from life into solitary cloisters to ponder the important questions that arise as they face challenging experiences and then, in a glorious moment of illumination, resolutions to life's timeless concerns are revealed. No, at least from God's perspective, the answer to the questions of our life experiences is the product of a divine process unfolding throughout our life.

The "what" of life always precedes the *how* of God. You always know what God has put on your heart or allowed in your life before you know how He intends to use it or bring it to pass. I have always said that, "When your desires connect with God's will, the universe conspires to help you achieve it." In order to fully understand the premise of this affirmation you must first understand an important term relative to God and His participation in your life situations, sovereignty.

The sovereignty of God is the biblical teaching that all things are under God's rule and control, and that nothing happens without His direction or permission. God works not just "some things" but "all things" according to the counsel of His own will (see Eph. 1:11). His purposes are all-inclusive and never thwarted (see Isa. 46:11); nothing takes Him by surprise. The sovereignty of God is not merely that God has the power and right to govern all things, but that He does so, always and without exception. In other words, God is not merely sovereign in principle, but sovereign in practice.

This sovereign process begins with us—His creation. Every thought we have is the end result of an experience He has allowed in our life. What we read and study and think about constantly, they are influenced by other thinkers and mentors permitted into our life, as well as the trials and joys of life. Gradually, ideas and questions begin to emerge as these life experiences evolve into serious challenges that bring pause in our life. Some ripen into convictions, while others over-ripen into discontentment, bitterness, and despair. In the end, they form what we call presuppositions. At some point in the process, we even dare to "think" about the appropriate response in the midst of all the confusion, conflict, and contemplation. Eventually, we get a breakthrough—a moment of clarity. Could all of this be God?

Everyone has presuppositions, a general set of beliefs, a grid through which we perceive everything that happens—a general belief about what is true. Our presuppositions form the basis for our values, and these values (good, bad, or indifferent) determine how we respond to life.

In The Beginning

What is it in mankind that insists on controlling his circumstances? It is the spiritual DNA given us by God. In the beginning He empowered man to have "dominion" and to "subdue" His creation. Prior to man's fall, he was created in the image of God having the supernatural ability to tap into God's consciousness. Man had the ability to discern God's mind concerning any and all situations that would interrupt His created world or anything that was intentionally left undone specifically for man to accomplish.

When man fell from grace in the Garden of Eden, he still had the inclination to know how to come out of a situation and control his environment—only now his attempts would be without the benefit of the consciousness of God and His *will* or should I say His *how.*

My objective in writing this book is to challenge your presuppositions concerning life and its many complex challenges and experiences. I want to raise the parameters of your thought life to a place where no matter what you have been through, or what you are going through, you can find peace in trusting the God of *how.* It is a spiritual place—that boundless realm of destiny where all things God has decreed IS possible and SHALL come to pass in your life. And reaffirm, that all things, whether good or bad, really do work together for your good—for those called according to God's purpose.

Part 1

Understanding Life's Trials

Chapter 1

THE TURNING POINT (STORY)

Savannah, Georgia—June 1991

HE'D JUST FLOWN IN from presenting a week long seminar in St. Thomas, Virgin Islands. Enroute home from the airport, he turns onto Bay Street from I-516. Driving through the historic district of downtown Savannah, he basked in the ease of living in this place of warm coastal breeze and meandering brick and cobblestone streets. And for the brief drive home, he chooses not to remember the tension between him and his wife before leaving for the seminar.

The man's name was William Clive Jamison II. Dusk was falling as he arrived in the driveway of his home. He immediately observed the signs of his worse fears. Something truly unspeakable had happened. The house was dark, and the daily newspapers had been collecting on the front lawn for several days. As he turns his key to open the front door, there is a knot in the pit of his stomach. There was no response to his greeting—hello, as it echoed through the naked entrance way; offering the first answers to some of the impending questions.

Little by little, from light switch to doorway, from room to room, his fears were becoming a reality. William collapsed to his knees in the middle of the living room, emotionally paralyzed by the shock of returning home to find it empty and filled with a disturbing silence. The common voices of his wife and children mute from the absence of their presence. Just a week earlier, he was sitting in that very living room with his thirteen-year-old son and eleven-year-old daughter at his feet watching their favorite sitcom, his wife, scurrying around the kitchen preparing dinner while making periodic remarks in response to the sitcom's dramatic moments. At that very moment his life was—perfect.

This would be the last perfect evening he would have with his family before leaving for St. Thomas the next morning. It would be the last evening he would spend with them as a family. One week later, after a remarkable week of lecturing, he returned home only to find his life dismantled and in utter disarray. He had always championed the cause of individuals experiencing personal abundance through the Spirit-filled life and striving to evolve to the next higher level of fulfillment in the areas of life, love and relationships. Indeed in the eyes of many he was the example of a loving husband and father, a dreamer, and a man living life fully in a successful ministry unfolding with each passing year. Yet, in one brief week, with one major decision (unknown to him), this man who was one of the most progressive voices in the arena of personal and spiritual empowerment—a champion of sorts, had been reduced to a victim.

He was a young up and coming leader. He was well known for his effervescent personality, and he was distinguished as a public speaker. Now kneeling on his empty living room floor with his travel-bag dropped and leaning against his laptop briefcase, he lifts his arms and places the palm of his hands against his forehead as if he was trying to keep it from falling off his neck. It was as if time was standing still waiting for his disbelief to catch up with the reality of the situation. His wife was following through on her desire to be free of the pressures of being the wife of a public figure. The expectations, the extensive travel, having to share her husband with the world had come to a head. She was now seeking a divorce. She was leaving a fifteen year marriage; taking his kids; ending the only reality known to William outside his ministry.

William collects his thoughts and proceeds to search for a note, a message—anything that would make sense out of what has happened. He slowly lifts from his knees and heads for the kitchen. The phone message recorder light is blinking. As William moves toward the message machine, there is heaviness in his chest. He senses that his worst fears will be confirmed upon pushing the play button on the answering machine. He hesitates, as if not playing the message would somehow not validate what is happening. With his heart beating so hard he could hear the pounding in his ear, William pushes play. The machine automated message plays, "You have one unheard message." The next voice he hears is a familiar one, it is his wife--Anna. With a crackle in her voice she says, "By the time you hear this message the kids and I will be back in south Florida. I'm sorry. I tried to make it work, but I can't live like this anymore. I've filed for divorce."

William immediately attempts to make contact with Anna to talk her out of the divorce. He was hoping that she would give them more time to make sense out of what went wrong and how they could possibly bring healing and repair to the situation. His attempts to reach her were unsuccessful. Day after day, for two weeks, he would call but to no avail. Anna would not return his call. Finally, William would once again pack his bags for a trip. This time it wouldn't be to speak to hundreds or thousands of eager listeners. This time he would be the uninvited, unwanted guest; imposing his unsolicited message of hope to a reluctant audience of one.

Ft. Lauderdale Beach, Florida

Sitting across the road from the beach in a small café on A1A sipping a freshly brewed cup of cappuccino, thoughts of the past few weeks' tumultuous events churned vigorously inside William's mind. His brain had become numb from thinking too much. With a dull headache, he pulls out his journal and begin to write, "Tearing through my heart and soul, there is an uneasiness, a gnawing in the pit of my stomach that seem to consume every ounce of my attention—haunting me as I attempt once again to make sense of it all. But how can I? This situation is more than I can bear. My relationship is in a shamble, I'm losing sleep, my work is suffering, and peace appears to ignore my deepest longing—my aching innate need for a moment of emotional repair."

All of this was perplexing and upsetting. For at that time William had already determined that divorce was an evil thing and the sooner this part of his life was behind him the better. Optimistically and secretly, of course—against the grim reality of a failed marriage, he was hoping for reconciliation. Eventually, his marriage did end, he toiled in disbelief. The man with the effervescent personality had lost his sense of humor and never seemed to laugh anymore. Perhaps the saddest thing was that he had lost his enthusiasm and focus toward life. It showed, emotionally, physically and spiritually.

As for his career, he hated it more bitterly than he could perhaps make clear. In his mind, the thought that maybe he became the wretched prisoner of his own making; pursuing his passion to inspire and change lives, oblivious to the downward spiral of his home-life. The thought that the cost of his success would be at the expense of his family oppressed him with an intolerable sense of guilt. He could get nothing into perspective. He had lost his sense of purpose. William was at that place where he was forced to confront the spiritual crisis of his out-of-balance life.

It is 9:37 p.m. The beach is nearly abandoned, only stragglers are left. The traffic is thinning and the noise level is lowering. The calm of the night slowly ushered in a sense of completion to yet another day of urgency and unrest. Still, William is feeling the anxious feelings of uncertainty. He finishes his cappuccino, pays his dinner bill and walked onto the sidewalk heading toward his car in a nearby parking garage. As William attempted to turn the corner and enter the garage, an unusual impression moved through his entire being.

It was as if he was overshadowed, immersed, and filled all in that same moment. With what, he did not know. All he knew was, without a sound or an audible voice; he was suddenly encouraged to walk the shoreline of the beach. So he did.

Crossing A1A, approaching the shoreline, William felt another impression. This time, he felt it was necessary to take off his shoes and socks and roll his pant leg bottom up. With his toes curling into the sand with each step, he began to walk the beach. Looking into the vastness of a dark night sky, after a while he began to feel the water from the receding waves brush against his ankles. He continued to walk. After a few minutes it occurred to him that he had been drawn farther into the ocean than where he'd began. The water was now nearing his knees. The ocean's undertow had been slowly pulling him out deeper with each cycle of recurring waves.

William's eyes had been focused upward at the stars; his ears were filled with the rhythmic sounds of ocean's breath. He was mesmerized. So much so, he was unaware that he no longer was consumed with the worries that had plagued him earlier. The peace that he'd longed for, but couldn't find, was unconsciously and suddenly upon him. Before William could read into the experience, the impression that overshadowed, immersed, and filled him almost an hour earlier began to gently echo—a still small voice from the deepest part of his human "self" saying, "This is how it feels to abide in My shadow. Here, you will experience an unknown peace; here you learn what it means to rest and be led by Me, God—the Spirit."

At this point William understood that things were about to change significantly in his life. He was about to turn another major corner in his life and God was watching. "Abiding in the Spirit," he said to himself. "But I've been teaching this principle most of my young life," he said to himself. He had no idea that the experiences that would follow over the next few years would mark a deeper connection with the presence of the Divine. He would embrace an invaluable truth that will change his life and ministry forever.

He remembered that throughout Scripture we are encouraged to "lean not to our own understanding." In all our ways acknowledge God, and He will direct our path—and he that dwells in the secret place of the most High shall abide under the shadow of the Almighty." Here, in these simple verses, lie the secret of all successful ventures and transitions in life.

He would soon discover, on this life-changing odyssey, that it is when we chose to make God a part of our very consciousness and when we chose to live our lives walking in His shadow, that we find true inner healing, refinement, and completeness. For William, the wake-up call to this reality happened the day he returned to Savannah. He began to discover a deeper relationship with God. He would now get to know another side of God—the God of *how*.

How singular is the thing called pleasure
and how curiously related to pain,
which might be thought to be the opposite of it...
yet he who pursues either is generally compelled to take the other;
their bodies are two but they are joined by the same head.
~ Socrates

Chapter 2

GOD WILL GIVE YOU MORE THAN YOU CAN HANDLE

AS A CHILD GROWING up in an old Pentecostal church in St. Marys, Georgia, I remember hearing for the first time the phrase: "God will never give you more than you can handle." I was in the primary Sunday school class of one of the "church mothers" who lived across the street from the church. After hearing it and eventual quoting it for years, at some point; it became a Christian-ism for me. I felt comforted knowing that God would never allow anything to happen to me that I could not "handle," whatever that meant in the world of Christendom. I am being somewhat cynical. But are we really aware of what that represent beyond the affirmation itself? Will I always be okay? Will things never be so terrible, as to crush me?

The real question that lurks in the back of our mind is, how much will this hurt? Whether it is emotional pain or physical pain, we all must prepare for the inevitable. Phillip Yancey, in his book, *Where Is God When It Hurts?,* had this to say, "When confronted with the facts, most of us will admit that pain—some pain, at least—serves a good and useful purpose. Apart from the warning system it provides, hidden dangers would shadow our everyday existence. Even more neglected, however, is the intimate connection that links pain and pleasure. The two sensations work together so closely they sometimes become almost indistinguishable."[1] Let's face it, no one equates pain with pleasure nor with purpose. So when the phrase "God will not give you more than you can handle" is used, it implies that there will be pain—unbearable pain which we expect to be minimized or avoided. The fact is, God sustains us to bear that which would, under normal circumstances and without God's assistance, not be able to handle or bear.

Paul, the Apostle, expressed the same sentiments:

> *Not that we are sufficient in ourselves to claim anything as coming from us, but our sufficiency is from God, who has made us sufficient to be.* (2 Corinthians 3:5)

Also,

> *And God is able to make all grace abound to you, so that having all sufficiency in all things at all times, you may abound in every good work.* (2 Corinthians 9:8)

These two verses of Scripture highlight the inability within ourselves to handle the unbearable weight of the many inevitable challenges we will face in life. God will allow overwhelming and potentially destructive circumstances to confront us and even come upon us. But it is because of His sufficiency that we are able to withstand being crushed or face total annihilation.

If you could handle every unbearable circumstance that presents itself, then there would be no need to transfer glory to God. In fact, how do you think Moses and the children of Israel felt when faced with Pharaoh and his army behind them and the Red Sea in front of them? Right! It was beyond their ability. It was more than they could bear. Moses heard a word from God and said, *Stand still and see the salvation of the Lord* (Exodus 14:13). Moses and the children of Israel knew that if it was left up to their own abilities and resources that they would die right where they stood.

What about King Jehoshaphat? He was warned that three kingdoms (the children of Ammon, Moab, and Seir), were coming against his kingdom. His military forces were not sufficient to withstand the mighty battalions of three great kingdoms. He knew it, so called for the entire kingdom, even the animals, to fast before God. If that wasn't bad enough, at the completion of the fast, God instructed Jehoshaphat not to engage his military forces in the fight. God's solution was for the king to bring his choir to the battle.

Really God? A choir? Yes! God knew how He was going to get glory out of the impossible situation confronting Jehoshaphat. Through obedience, proper positioning, and triumphant praise, God's sufficiency sustained King Jehoshaphat and Judah (his kingdom). It was on the cliff of Ziz that God confirmed:

> *You shall not need to fight in this battle: set yourselves, stand still, and see the salvation of the Lord with you. And Jehoshaphat bowed his head with his face to the ground: and all Judah and the inhabitants of Jerusalem feel before the Lord, worshipping the Lord* (2 Chronicles 20:16-18).

God *will* allow more on you than you can handle. Because it is at this point you become aware of the omnipotent and inexhaustible power of God. It is in the impossible settings in

> God's sufficiency will allow overwhelming and potentially destructive circumstances to confront us.

life that you have no other choice but to transfer glory to God. In Jehoshaphat's case God set a divine "ambushment" against the enemy and utterly destroyed them. So it will be with you, God is orchestrating a divine *how* on your behalf. Your divine *how* may be in the form of an unlikely career you are considering, a position you're applying for that appear to be out of reach, a financial burden weighing heavy upon you, a physical illness or condition you think you can't beat. Whatever your impossible or unbearable situation may be, know that the God of *how* has got your back! He won't let you down. *With men this is impossible; but with God all things are possible.* (Matthew 19:26 KJV)

For William, in Chapter 1, divorce would prove to be one of many difficult situations that will come to test this statement of faith. I remember quite a few years ago even writing those words to a childhood friend of mine who was going through a difficult time. I felt like it was in the Bible. It seemed like it should be in the Bible. It sounded theologically sound and comforting. For years, like many Christians, I had always quoted but had never actually check to see if it was in the Bible. It is a common practice, if you hear it in church from credible leaders and seasoned parishioners it must be true.

But then one day as I was in my study preparing for a speaking engagement I had a run-in with the truth. I discover that the whole "God won't give you more than you can handle" business was an error. And that Satan has twisted that one and we've bought it.

The truth is, the Bible doesn't talk about giving or not giving us more than we can handle. To embrace that at face value would lend itself to the assumption that you will never come under unbearable pressures in life and secondly, that you are responsible for the *how* of navigating through such pressures. There is no getting around the pressures and sufferings associated with life transitions. According to Yancey, we meet suffering people in every school, in every church, in every public building, as well as in every hospital. All of us will one day join them. As I've listened to what they have to say, I have come up with four "frontiers" where every suffering person will do battle:

> "The frontiers of fear, helplessness, meaning, and hope. Our response to suffering depends largely on the outcome of our struggle in those frontiers."[2]

The verse that Christians so often confuse with this phrase is 1 Corinthians 10:13:

> *No temptation has overtaken you that is not common to man. God is faithful, and he will not let you be tempted beyond your ability, but with the temptation he will also provide the way of escape, that you may be able to endure it.*

The key word here is "temptation." We are promised here by the apostle Paul that God will not allow us to be "tempted beyond our ability." Temptation is very different from the vast, exhaustive list in life of anything that could happen to us. God doesn't say He won't give us what we can't handle. He says we won't be tempted beyond our ability.

What is our ability? Well, the second half of the verse, I think, helps answer that question: "But with the temptation he will also provide the way of escape, that you may be able to endure it." We are confronted with and responsible for the questions surrounding the challenges and pressures that are a direct result of choices we've made in our life. Yet still, our ability is tied to the way of escape—to the God of *how*. God obligates Himself to the *how* of any situation beyond our abilities. We are offered an exit door with every temptation and every pressure. It is through that exit door, in part, that we receive the ability to resist the temptation. We cannot endure a temptation unless we escape it. Our ability is also measured by our maturity in Christ and our reliance upon the Holy Spirit, among other things.

God certainly does allow us to experience more than we can handle, though. Jesus was given more than He could humanly handle. He was beaten and crucified to death. He died without sin, however, because while He was tempted, He knew the way of escape.

Over thirty-three years in ministry, I have counsels hundreds, even thousands of individuals whose life story would validate my position. I could refer to a parent losing a child. A woman I knew who had watched three of her babies die, one after another. Years later her marriage ended in divorce and she was diagnosed with pancreatic cancer.

Was this woman's loss enough for her to handle? We say, "God doesn't give us more than we can handle," and we lie to ourselves. Was burying three infants, losing her husband, and being diagnosed with cancer more than this woman could handle? I think so. She fell into a deep and intense depression. She couldn't handle it. She wasn't meant to handle it.

God will inevitably allow us to experience more than we can handle—the death of a parent, or a spouse. Perhaps it is watching a life-long dream wither away and die, or the man or woman who experiences the pain of extended unemployment ultimately leading to them being indigent and homeless. Or even the realization that you have been wasting your life and have nothing to show for it. Any of these things are more than we can handle and that's the point.

Christianity is not the guarantee of an easy life, but the abundant life. It makes us uncomfortable to think about suffering loss and God allowing that loss. Dr. Mark D. Hanby, an author, pastor, international speaker and teacher, spoke of suffering and loss as a part of the process of becoming a vessel for God's use. He further states that, "We discover that the process of becoming a vessel for God is akin to the process of molding a clay vessel on a potter's wheel. As we are fashioned and reshaped through spinning disorientation, we can choose to stay on the wheel and be molded into God's workmanship, or we can eject ourselves from the process and refuse the purpose and peace of God."[3]

Job has always been a major focus when referring to Christian suffering and perseverance. He too was placed on the potter's wheel. It shaped him for the success God ultimately intended for his life. Yes, it is tough to fathom such faith under fire. He lost his children, his wealth, his friends, and ultimately the betrayal of his wife. As one read this historical reference of trust and endurance, you can't help but realize that God wants us to cling to Him. He wants us to hold onto Him for dear life because, without Him, we would drift aimlessly away into misdirection and despair.

Make no mistake, we will suffer greatly at different seasons and times in our life, and it is because of our sufferings and through our sufferings that we discover not

> God obligates Himself to provide a resolution, or a way of escape that you may be able to endure.

only the all sufficiency of the God of *how* but we discover that suffering is a key component in the process of "becoming." We are all born with the innate potential of becoming whatever God has predetermined us to become. But more so, that we first aspire to Christlikeness. Paul wrote, for example:

> *I want to know Christ and the power of his resurrection and the fellowship of sharing in his sufferings, becoming like him in his death.* (Philippians 3:10)

Knowing Christ and sharing in His sufferings positions you to experience the molding, shaping, and directing hand of God. I accept the idea that God will, perhaps at more than one point in my life, allow me to experience such pain and loss that I will be broken under the weight of it. The key word is broken not annihilated. Paul continues to address this in his second letter to the church of Corinth:

> *We are hard-pressed on every side, yet not crushed; we are perplexed, but not in despair; persecuted, but not forsaken; struck down, but not destroyed—always carrying about in the body the dying of the Lord Jesus, that the life of Jesus also may be manifested in our mortal flesh.* (2 Corinthians 4:8-11 NKJV)

Many new Christians and even some veteran believers come into the fellowship of the church body to escape hell (fire insurance) and in doing so they also assume they can escape hardships in life. This is why many people become disillusion and frustrated with religion. When life becomes too tough to manage they resolve that religion doesn't work. Well, the fact of the matter is, religion doesn't work. God has not called us to religion; He has called us into relationship with Him. When you are in relationship with God, you won't buy into the lie any longer of naively believing that there is some magic limit or glass ceiling on suffering. There isn't, and we demean the power of Christ's sufferings when we assume there is.

Hanby refers to suffering and the baptism by fire as synonymous. According to Luke 3:16-17, one of the fundamental doctrines of the Church is the baptism of fire. We understand baptism in water and the baptism of the Holy Spirit. John baptized in water. Jesus baptized you with the Holy Spirit and with fire. The fan of the fire is in God's hand. He separates the chaff from the wheat and burns it with unquenchable fire. God created the smith who blows the coals. He knows how much heat is needed in your life to make you what you have to be so He can use you for His glory. If you couldn't take the fire (with His assistance), God wouldn't blow on it."[4]

It seems that trials come in certain seasons, and our suffering within those trials comes in waves with occasional short breaks in between. They sometimes leave people asking the question: "Where was God when I needed Him?" or "Why does God allow such things to happen?" We must fully understand that suffering is not "God being mean" or putting something bad on us. God knows what must be in us before we can be trusted with the future he has for us. So we need to be successful in the process of our suffering. When fiery hardships and trials came, James the preacher said "Count it all joy!" (James 1:2)[5]

I recently preached a sermon on the matter. The scripture passage I chose was James 1: 1-12. I outlined four points taken from those powerful and introspective verses that help answer the question, "Why am I going through this?"

Triumph Involves Attitude

"Consider it a sheer gift, friends, when tests and challenges come at you from all sides. You know that under pressure, your faith-life is forced into the open and shows its true colors. So don't try to get out of anything prematurely. Let it do its work so you become mature and well-developed, not deficient in any way." (James 1: 2-4, the Message)

You must be kidding? People should be joyful in the midst of trials as if receiving a gift? Absolutely, it does not mean that we have to be blissful about the trials we must face, but the Bible makes it clear that Christians should consider it a gift which should sustain your joy because God does have a purpose. Verses 2-4 state that the trials we face serve to test our faith for the purpose of development. Testing leads to perseverance. Perseverance leads to maturity.

Triumph Involves Faith

"If any of you lacks wisdom, let him ask God who gives liberally and without reproach, and it will be given to him. But let him ask in faith, without doubting, for he who doubts is like the wave of the sea, driven and tossed by the wind. For let not that man suppose that he will receive anything from the Lord, he is a double-minded man, unstable in all his ways." (James 1: 5-8, NKJV)

As I said earlier, the Bible never promised that Christian people would not suffer trials. He never promised to remove trials from our lives. He does promise that He will lead His people through trials. Trust me, I get it. Nothing is as frightening as the unknown when you're going through a trial and faced with uncertainty. However, he expects his children to pray and seek Him during those times. When

His people seek Him, they must have faith and believe that God will not only be with them but, he will also lead them through it.

Triumph Involves Humility

"The brother in humble circumstances ought to take pride in his high position, but the one who is rich should take pride in his low position because he will pass away like a wild flower, for the sun rises with a scorching heat and withers the plant; its blossom falls and its beauty is destroyed. In the same way, the rich man will fade away even while he goes about his business." (James 1: 8-11, The Bible)

Triumph from the terrors of tragedy would be impossible without God. We live in an immoral, harsh world. When declaring a bold proclamation of triumph, God must be exalted and glory must be transferred to Him, for it is only through His grace and power, not human strength that we persevere through trials and tragedies.

Triumph Involves Blessing

"Blessed is the one who perseveres under trial because, having stood the test, that person will receive the crown of life that the Lord has promised to those who love him." (James 1:12, NIV)

Trials creep in our life like an intruder seeking to steal away our peace, prosperity, and well-being. But within the experiences of trials we have discovered a deeper and more profound meaning. Still there is another benefit. Consider trials not only as a joy but also a blessing. In the book of Job, the refining fire of trials excavates and polishes our hidden beauty and value that lie beneath the crust of human nature. The writer says:

> *But He knows the way that I take; when He has tested me (When you have been through the fire), I shall come forth as gold.* (Job 23:10, NKJV)

Anytime you hear the word triumph it is always associated with the favorable end results of a fight or a battle. Kay Arthur, author and co-founder of Precept Ministries, says that "the power for victory is there if you listen to and submit in faith to the Captain of the host, King Jesus. Like any military operation, you must stay in constant communication—in essence, stay in the Word of God so you can know the will of your Commander, and pray without ceasing, and obey fully His commands.

You must concentrate on your forces—and your forces are all the promises of God. Strengthen your security by believing those promises, for in your knowledge of Him, God has broadened and strengthened your shield of faith. By this time, you will have gained good intelligence about the tactics of your enemy. You know he will come at you with lies and accusations. You know his tactics are deadly, because he's a murderer as well as a liar, a deceiver.

Remember all you've learned of your enemy, and be prepared accordingly. Don't be caught off guard by his surprise attacks. And never forget that the end of the battle, the demise of the enemy, has already been foretold. It is as certain as God—and even the devil knows it, according to Revelation 12:12. You are on the winning side. Hold your position...and advance."[6]

Unhappy memories are persistent. They're specific, and it's the details that refuse to leave us alone. Though a happy memory may stay with you just as long as one that makes you miserable, what you remember softens over time. What you recall is simply that you were happy, not necessarily the individual moments that brought about your joy.

But the memory of something painful does just the opposite. It retains its original shape, all bony fingers and pointy elbows. Every time it returns, you get a quick poke in the eye or jab in the stomach. The memory of being unhappy has the power to hurt us long after the fact. We feel the injury anew each and every time we think of it.
~ Cameron Dokey

Chapter 3

VISITING THE PAST—BUT NOT FOR TOO LONG (STORY)

St. Marys, Georgia—Summer 1975

WILLIAM CLIVE JAMISON II, the boy, lived in a small town a few miles north of the Georgia-Florida state lines. His family called him Fess for short because he loved school and it was short for professor. The small town (St. Marys) wasn't anything like its neighboring cities: Kingsland and Woodbine. What made St. Marys special was that there was only one way in and one way out. You couldn't drive through the small town unless you own a boat to cross the signature feature of the town—the St. Marys River. Lining the river banks were shrimp boats, fishing docks, and piers to further distinguish this small town from all the other surrounding cities.

The days were filled with industrial workers and paper mill plant workers going to and from work or work assignments. The local children would be in school and the stay-at-home mothers would be doing house chores and preparing for their families to return home in the evening.

The nights were silent in St. Marys. There were no malls to walk through, no movies to go to, and no clubs to meet up with friends and check girls out. There were no big city distractions to lure families away from the dinner table at 6:00 PM and separate them for the evening. For William, the nights in this small town were the most amazing. It was the only time for him to steal away under the moonlight and dream beyond his present reality. Life at that time, as William knew it, was quite simple. Soon things in his small world would change and set some events into play that would alter the course of his life.

William, His Dad, Religion, and God

Awakening from the typical sweltering heat of a southeast Georgia night, William kicks the bed covers off and hangs one leg over the side swinging it—attempting to find a cool current blowing from the electric fan below at the foot of his bed-frame. Brushing the beads of sweat from his brow, he takes a deep breath of air that comes close to body temperature. Although this was that dawning of a typical summer day in the South, this was not a typical day for William. The night before he'd had his first kiss from the girl he had a crush on since attending Matilda Harris Elementary School (the school where all the black kids attended during the times of racial segregation). Sixteen years old, at Camden County High School, and becoming significant in the life of the girl of his dreams—it was as if the planets were lining up and the universe was cooperating with a master plan. Everything in his world was flowing well.

As to be expected, he started his day on a mental high. With the memory of kissing Alicia Barber, the most beautiful girl, in the county, nothing could ruin his day; so he thought. School was out for summer break and a few of the neighborhood teenagers had planned to meet at the Crooked River State Park. This, he reasoned, would be another opportunity to see her again. The more time he spent with Alicia, the more he sensed that she was being drawn closer to him. Maybe, if the last month of summer went well, they could be high school sweethearts by the beginning of the new school year. Everything seemed to be falling into place. Then it happened. The sound of his father's voice calling him signaled that something was wrong.

William jumped out of bed and hurried to the living room where his father was waiting. As he turned the corner from the hallway and entered the living room, he observed the signs of the impending doom to his plans for the day. His dad was sitting in his recliner with his Bible on the table next to him and a grim look in his eye. Someone saw Alicia and him kissing and thought it was his duty to inform the Good Rev. Jamison Sr. Living in a small town, everyone knows everyone. To some degree, growing up in such a societal microcosm has its advantages. But for William, on this day, an advantage would be very difficult to fathom.

"I understand you were with a certain young lady last night in a compromising situation," his father said. "No!" William replied. His father responded, "Don't lie to me!" "But Dad" he replied, "it wasn't a compromising situation; I was with Alicia Barber you know her family. Alicia and I met downtown at the Waterfront Pavilion. I was there with some friends watching the fishermen maneuver their boats into the docks after a long day. I didn't know she was there until later on in the evening. She and our next door neighbor, Paula, came there together. We began to talk and lost track of time. Before long it was getting dark so I asked if I could walk her home. I've always liked her, a lot. This was the first time I have ever had the opportunity to spend time with her and tell her how I feel about her. We like each other Dad. Once we entered the driveway to her house, I asked if I could kiss her goodnight and she said yes! It was my first kiss Dad! I didn't know that I'd done anything wrong."

At that moment, his father stood to his feet and verbally scolded William. Flinging his arms in the air, he gave him chapter and verse of his position in the community as a minister and how his children are expected to be an example of discipline. It was as if he was preaching a sermon of damnation to an audience of one. In his conclusion, he forbade William to date until he felt like it was appropriate.

William turned away in anger and under his voice, cursing the day he was ever born into a minister's home. As he stormed away in disbelief of what had just transpired, the Good Rev. William Jamison Sr. issued a final judgment in his authoritative, righteous indignant flurry, "By the way, you're grounded for the rest of the summer!" William's heart sunk, and with great disdain for how being a preacher's kid interfered with his experiencing what seemed normal for life as a teenager; he swore he'd never become a minister. After all, how could being in love and an innocent kiss offend God, yet alone, threaten the reputation of a minister's family.

In high school William's friends would secretly peered in the windows of the Main Street Church of God (aka holy rollers), who spoke in tongues, sometimes screaming with a frightening ecstatic look on their faces and falling to the floor writhing and jerking. That seemed, to his friends, particularly close to the mysterious spells they heard about cast on people by the South Carolina witch-doctor referred to as Dr. Buzzard.

It was difficult as a teenager growing up in a minister's home, in the God-fearing, faith-healing, end-of-the-world-is-at-hand South Georgia. Yet still, William absorbed the Southern obsession with "place," and "place" especially in a small town can seem to be somehow an extension of self. However, now living as a grown man in South Florida, He never has that belonging sensation. In his mind he is the awe tourist, delighted to have made this brief escape, which is his adult life.

"Get back in this house boy!" his father shouted. "No!" William replied. He passed his mother while exiting the patio. With a soft sweet voice she called out to him, "William!" He could hear the concern in her tone. He stopped and turned around. Looking into her face with tears in his eyes, he asked, "Why did you marry him?" "I love you mom, but I can't deal with him anymore."

William and his father's relationship could best be described as tumultuous to say the least. Being raised in a strict Pentecostal preacher's home wasn't an ideal situation for a teenager during the early seventies. Main stream denominations back then were intolerable of what they contended were "worldly lusts."

When things calmed down a bit William asked his mother if he could go for a ride. He rolled his dark blue, banana-seat bike out of the small laundry room connected to the rear of the family garage. He mounted his bike as he had always done—pretending it to be the Yamaha dirt-bike that he'd dreamed of one day owning. He rode through his hometown of St. Marys, Georgia. About eight blocks away from the downtown riverfront, his young legs finally grew weary so he stopped. He noticed a side road which led to a pathway. So he got off his bike and began to walk his bike down this road.

Once to the grassy pathway, William laid his bike down and walked through the narrow trail. After walking about five hundred feet, the grassy path with a mixture of reeds and wetland plants, open into a beautiful small body of water. It was one of the many saltwater wetlands that connected to the St. Marys River. He remembered overhearing stories from the neighborhood boys about a place they called Major Moore's Marsh. It was a place where they would go to swim during those hot South Georgia summers. Maybe this was the mysterious secret place where his neighborhood friends would escape to. He was never allowed, so he was never invited. He was a preacher's kid. Such excursions without proper notice or adult supervision were not tolerated.

He noticed a flat-spot amidst the grass and reeds as if someone had matted the tall blades down for a place to camp. Walking toward the spot with an analytical eye, watchful of anything that may seem suspicious, William cautiously inspected his surroundings to ensure he was alone and that nothing was near that would harm him. He sat down, that is when he saw an old wet Bible ripped in two halves. The loose pages were scattered all over that marshland. The one halve of the Bible was opened to a passage of a book called Jeremiah. It read, "Before I formed you in the womb I knew you; before you were born I sanctified you; I appointed you a prophet to the nations." It was a scripture he'd heard his father recite in church on occasions.

Next to the ripped half Bible was a torn page from the other half, which he never found. Its contents were everywhere—in the marsh, spread all along the grassy edges of the wetland. He picked up the soiled, wrinkled, torn page. He never saw the book of the Bible it came from, but it read, "I will never leave you nor forsake you—the Lord is my helper; I will not fear. What can man do to me?" This he also heard his father quote many times. But this time, something was different.

Reading those sacred words together himself, he felt as if a voice deep within his inner most personal self was speaking the words into his mind. Unaware of the significance of this moment, he was scared. At that moment, he dropped the pages and looked around to see if someone was playing a trick on him. No-one was there, at least no-one that he could see. Startled, he raced back through the grassy, reed-filled pathway toward his bike without looking back. His heart was pounding so hard, as though it wanted to jump out of his chest. He hurriedly rode his bike home. He thought to himself, "That was spooky, way too spooky for me." Little did he know, it wasn't spooky, it was a calling—an intimate commission from the Divine.

That bike ride home over thirty years ago was the beginning of William's lifelong interest in God and the purpose he would serve in this world—an interest that led him to study people—their behavior, life management, philosophy and religion. Although he grew up in a preacher's home, William, because of strained father-son relationship, until that point had not bought into what he considered the 'religious hype.'

He embraced the belief that there was an intelligent, powerful, and divine being. With his young innocent mind, he believed that this magnificent divine being created and manages the details of the universe. He believed in God. Even at such a young age William believed that if God was love, then He would desire a relationship.

To William, religion was cold and impersonal with a mandated "Things-To-Do or Be Rejected" list. In his heart he knew that there was much more to knowing and serving God.

That day marked the beginning of the many pivotal moments in life. And William would be shaped by what he now calls "divinely-orchestrated defining moments."

I believe God made me for a purpose, but he also made me fast.
And when I run, I feel His pleasure.
~ Eric Liddell, Olympian and Christian missionary

Chapter 4

DRIVEN BY PRESSURE OR GOD'S PLEASURE

THE FIRST TIME I watched *Chariots of Fire* was back in the eighties. I was a freshman at Lee College in Cleveland, Tennessee. As a young man studying for the ministry, this movie changed my life. Filled with so many thought provoking moments, it was when Eric Liddell spoke his famous quote in the film, four words that stood out: God, purpose, pleasure, and me.

God Made Me for His Pleasure?

The weirdest, most fascinating, and shuddering combination of thoughts started filling my head. I began to believe in an extraordinary future. My belief began to stretch out into my faith in God's ability through me and optimism was birthed inside of me. It hasn't stopped growing since. Author, Eric Fellman, said that optimism is one of the foundations of spiritual potential. Optimism that becomes hope. Hope is best seen rising out of despair, and despair is the everyday reality of many people who find themselves behind in the game of life, sometimes even before the games have really begun.[1]

In Chapter 3 we see William the teenager. As a high schooler, looking into his future, he was at a cross-road. Experiencing father-son pressures, the simple innocent pleasures birthed in womb of young love, and trying to figure out what to do with his life beyond the moment William discovers more about the "why" of his existence. He could be driven either by the pressure of life or by the pleasure God wanted to experience through him.

Vince Lombardi once said, "Once you agree upon the price you and your family must pay for success, it enables you to ignore the minor hurts, the opponent's pressure, and the temporary failures."

Life is about seeking and working toward a balance between our desires and God's purpose for our success in life.

Regular pressures of life seem agonizing at times because there are so may unforeseen variables. Constant variables can be distressing unless you understand God's purpose and pleasure for your life as you face life's challenges. The world we live in is filled with conflicting motives as it relate to pursuing purpose. As you strive to please God and reconcile your mind with His mind, your motives may often be misconstrued by the pressures of the vast worldly influences we must contend with daily. Because of this contention you may assume at times, you are not making any progress. And based on your limited natural judgment, not knowing much about God's higher plans for you, you don't know what is true. You don't know whom to believe. Also, you don't trust your experiences because they don't quite prove out in daily life anymore.

Life is about seeking and working toward a balance between your desires and conflicts, and God's purpose and His pleasure for your life. Fellman further suggests that "Life is a journey, and doing life well is about making as much progress as possible toward your goals. Our destination is a higher existence in the next life, but in this life we're always progressing—never standing still, never finishing."² Paul the Apostle said it best:

> *Not that I have already attained, or am already perfect, but I press on, that I may lay hold of that for which Christ Jesus has also laid hold of me. Brethren, I do not count myself to have apprehended; but one thing I do, forgetting those things which are behind and reaching forward to those things which are ahead, I press toward the goal for the prize of the upward call of God in Christ Jesus.* (Philippians 3:12-14 KJV)

Paul validates the proper attitude toward spiritual development as well as personal achievement. Progress requires that we don't allow the pressures of this world to stagnate our movement. We must reach forward and press toward our goals and God's purpose.

Like William, we are all trying to find out where we fit in the scheme of things; especially when life seems to not make much sense. Then God comes along and rocks our world with "His purpose" and "His pleasure" for our life. It takes a while to figure out this purpose and pleasure thing with God. For whatever reason, at first glance it is difficult to trust it. After all, we live in a world vast in influences and motives.

Problem solving, feeling guilty, and the safety of self-reliance— these feel more natural than depending on a relationship with God that is still in process. It is human nature to sacrifice true purpose and peace on the altar of self-reliance. But according to God, these qualities aren't a part of His plan for us. When you take a look at the Abraham's experience, to the natural mind, it was impossible for God's promise of a child to Sarah's barren womb and both Abraham's and Sarah's old age to be fulfilled. But Abraham didn't dwell on any such impossibility. According to Paul, the patriarch gave no thought to how God would keep His promise. He simply "considered not" and he "patiently endured."

When God is in the process of raising your faith level and nurturing His purpose in your life, he first puts you in a place where all of your human resources are exhausted. It is a place where human dependence on temporal means ends and the supernatural potential of God begins. It is place where He closes the door to all human reasoning, bypassing every means of a rational deliverance, and stress comes upon you like creeping paralysis–slowly infiltrating every crevice of unbelief until it has saturated your thought life with irrational images of failure and defeat.

It is at that place of stress that our faith is not only tested but developed. Stress if not subdued by faith can be lethal to our forward movement. Stress is like a pathogen (an infectious agent that causes disease) that attacks and weakens our ability to experience God's pleasure. Every day, there is a continuous flow of decisions we make, large or small, to give into pressure or pleasure.

Without a doubt, we live in an imperfect world, and in this world Satan has intensified his desire and strategies to sift us of our dreams and destiny. He uses every weakness against us to keep us susceptible to guilt, insecurities, and stress—even though, we were originally made for joy, peace, and rest. So often we are tempted to be overwhelmed by our own shortcomings, instead of, totally focusing on how great our God is:

> *He who is able to do far more abundantly beyond all*
> *that we ask or think, according to the power that works*
> *within us…* (Ephesian 3:20 NKJV).

Yet still, we struggle with the natural desire to have a preferred formula, check boxes, or some "4 Simple Steps" to find happiness, fulfillment and purpose. We resort to making decisions that could worsen our struggle. Our plans eventually are foiled by unforeseen setbacks, and we are left with a broken spirit and a sorrowful heart. Does this sound familiar?

Thank God, He is faithful toward us, pointing us to an unbeaten path with Him, a break from who we were yesterday, and a new way of thinking. We can put pressure on ourselves, and we force change apart from God's design and purpose. The results, though, aren't long lasting and hold hidden costs, beyond the upfront price. In contrast, God woos us to visibly experience His divine purpose for our life as the world looks on and experience His pleasure *from within*. It's the kind of change that is real, when we dare to believe we were created for God's pleasure—and take new steps to discover what that means.

Author Vance Havner once said, "We cannot change our heart but we can change our mind, and when we change our mind, then God will change our heart." This statement drew me closer to the reality of authentic change and God's pleasure in me if I followed through with the necessary changes. First, God wants us to love Him thoughtfully—*"love Him with our mind."* In essence, He wants us to think through life's situations with the benefit of His counsel, not just doing life without thinking. Secondly, He wants us to love Him passionately—*"with all our heart and all our soul."* He wants us to love Him passionately because He loves us passionately. Thirdly, He says, He want us to love Him practically—*"love Me with all your strength,"* with your abilities.

As awesome as God is, the truth is that, even though God created the entire world and the universe, and He created you; there are three things God does not have unless you give them to Him. He doesn't have your attention unless you give it to Him. That is loving God with your mind. He doesn't have your affection unless you give it to Him. That is loving God with your heart and your soul. And God doesn't have your ability, unless you give it to Him. That is loving God with your strength. Whenever

> When God is in the process of developing your faith, He allows you to travel a path to a place where your human abilities and resources are exhausted.

you take the things God has given to you, and you give them back to God—that is when you experience God's pleasure.

Life's true north—its navigation system and its greatest pleasure are found in God. Psalm 16:11 reveals that:

> *You (God) will make known to me the path of life; in Your presence is fullness of joy; in Your right hand there are pleasures forever.*

His navigation system does not fail. His fullness of joy cannot be improved. And His pleasures are inexhaustible. If we are ever privy to such honors, we owe it all to the presence of God, not the accomplishments of man.

Believe it or not, God's pleasure undoubtedly sends super-shock waves through the universe. But, they can be sensed by the spiritually sensitive human heart of His children, and if they are looking and care to know His thoughts, His purpose, and His pleasure, they may feel it. At the same time, I wonder how many of God's children go about their lives without ever stopping to experience His delight. I have been guilty at times in my life of missing God's pleasure and purpose because I was too busy or distracted to notice Him in my situation. I thought I could direct my own steps. I was wrong, and I missed God in the process.

I remember, for a brief season, when I was young in ministry, I didn't actually apply myself to doing what God had in fact created me to do. And though there was enjoyment and reward in doing other tasks and pursuing other goals, I never felt God's pleasure in doing those things as I do when I preach God's Word. And, knowing that now, I would not have spent so much time doing anything other than that which brings my Father the most pleasure because there is no greater joy in this life than in feeling that you are doing the very thing that God put you on this earth to do.

So you must ask yourself, what has God put me on this earth to do? It may not be preaching God's Word but rather owning your own business, designing clothes, producing music, creating art, constructing buildings, or educating young minds. It really doesn't matter what it is, as long as, you know that you are doing the very thing God has created you to do.

At the same time, if you find yourself at the point of discovery where God has allowed you to engage in a career or a job that represent a pit-stop to your ultimate destiny, we are required to perform our tasks as unto the Lord. I believe even in this we can experience God's pleasure. There is a saying that I embrace whole heartedly, "Do what you can do, until it is time to do what you are supposed to do." Be spiritually sensitive to know the difference.

The pressures of life can be strong. At times, driving you to make decisions without acknowledging the importance of God's input concerning His plans for you. Don't give in to the pressure, and don't settle for anything less than what God intended.

We may have a good reason for giving in, settling, and being sad about what has happened to us, but self-pity is the wrong way to respond to it. According to William Hines, college professor and author, "When we engage in self-pity we are in a position of pride and mistrust. Pride in that we say through our self-pity, 'I am too good for this,' or. 'I don't deserve this.' It is mistrust in that we are not trusting in the providence of God. God is the ruler of the universe, and we must trust that what He allows, He allows for a good reason. We may not understand what the reason is, but we do understand that what He wants us to do now is trust Him and go on with life in obedience to Him.[3]

Here what the Prophet Isaiah says:

> *Come, buy wine and milk without money and without cost. Why spend money on what is not bread, and your labor on what does not satisfy? Listen, listen to me, and eat what is good.* ***And delight yourself in abundance.*** *(*Isaiah 55:2 NKJV)

Dr. Timothy Clinton, president of the American Association of Christian Counselors and publisher of the award-winning *Christian Counseling Today* magazine, wrote on "The Affection of the Pursuing God: A Love That Will Not Let Me Go." He asked, whether you ever noticed that once you hit bottom with no options or avenues of escape, it seems, as if, you are living in the worst of times and the best of times? How can that be? Perhaps it is because, in one sense, as bad as things may seem, the only way to go is up.

Even in your darkest moment, if Christ dwells in you, there is a song deep in your soul that sings, "He will make a way. Someday, everything's going to be changed because God will make a way for me."

The mind may forget, but the heart always remembers Him who said, "I am the Lord thy God, which brought thee out of the land of Egypt: open thy mouth wide, and I will fill it." (Psalms 81:10 KJV)

The downward spiral toward the loss of heart can leave us feeling stranded, abandoned, and in despair—with little desire or ability to help ourselves. But do not lose heart. God always has His way. You are in the sight of the Pursuer God. We don't pursue Him as much as He pursues us. That's probably why you're reading this book. He has been gently calling you. What happens next is up to you.[4]

Be driven by God's pleasure and discover the transforming power of a surrendered life. You will come to trust Him with the experiences of your past, the precious things of your present, and your hopes for the future.

Most people are other people. Their thoughts are someone else's opinions, their lives a mimicry, their passions a quotation.
~ Oscar Wilde

Chapter 5

THE IMAGE SABBATICAL: TAKING A BREAK FROM WHO YOU THINK YOU ARE (STORY)

Story Prologue

TYPICALLY, YOU HAVE DERIVED your image or identity through form. Ego is form-identification. Your ego is vested in the "I am". It chooses to anchor itself with labels. It identifies with the thoughts "I am a Pentecostal," "I am a minister," "I am successful," "I am good" and "I am right". Unfortunately, who you are cannot be known through thinking. Who you truly are comes from a God consciousness apart from man-made ideals. Free from cultural prejudices and social adaptations. Although they are the initial tools used to shape our image, they are in fact the substitute images of fallen nature. In the image of God we were created, and in the image of God shall we return if we are to discover who we really are and fulfill His plan for our life.

Image was an important part of upward mobility and acceptance in William's previous world of ministry, and perhaps others as well.

There was a time when he was forever committed to the cause and position of his denomination. But times and things were changing in the world he was called to make a difference in. He loved pastoring. When he preached on Sunday, taught at mid-week Bible study, and counseled people he felt his life had a higher meaning and purpose.

Attending state conventions and international general assemblies were the highlight of his year. State convention was a time when ministers and members alike would come from near and far to one place, at one time in a predetermine city in their perspective states around the United States to fellowship, attend seminars, and worship together for one week each year. The international general assemblies were similar, but they were held every four years. Pastors, ministers, members, and state and international officials would gather from every corner of the world—tens of thousands of the denomination's constituency would gather and it was not short of amazing.

In such an environment, one can see how easy it would be to fall victim to the demands of an organization with such collective camaraderie and worldwide influence. Perhaps, some of the imagery is of our own individual doing, or not. But the spirit of "image" is significantly nurtured by the desire of promotion through the ranks of ministry and the acceptance, notoriety, and honor bestowed upon those who do adhere to and develop it well.

William had done so and he was on the fast track to a very promising future with the organization. Still, he had unanswered questions about functions, protocols, and doctrinal positions that seem archaic and irrelevant to times we live in. Could he remain committed to the organization he was born and raised in despite his conflict? Was he called to be among others who felt the same but had not yet spoken up? Or was it his destiny to transition out—to find his place elsewhere?

While he didn't set out to be controversial, he thought it was better than simply being comfortable with what was no longer working in his life. He had consulted with other non-denominational ministers not associated with his denomination that gave valuable insight and counsel. His desire was not to stir up confusion, but rather to follow his own path. The fundamental differences jeopardized William the man and the image he had come to enjoy. His questions and ultimate departure from the organization set the stage for an uncontrollable downward spiral in ministry. One thing he would discover is that if your friends, family, and ministry associates aren't knit into the fabric of your life in a healthy way, social isolation is inevitable.

The Man He Used To Be Is Dying

Atlanta, Georgia—1993

It's been two years since William's life began to unravel. The person he thought he was has been challenged through the whole process. Before he could begin to understand what he was to become and how God would do it, he needed to fully understand his present identity crisis. His whole image as a minister was sculpted by a religious organization and a family name which included a circle of associates that together became a source of influence and affirmation which he became dependent upon to validate him as a man, a husband, a father, and a minister.

William resigned his ministry from the denomination of his youth prior to the divorce. God was leading him in another direction which did not fit within parameters of some of the legalistic views he had come to disagree with as he trained, and developed into a well versed expositor of theology and a progressive pastoral minister. For the first time in his life, William had no denomination to depend on—no family name to build upon—and the dark cloud of a broken marriage hanging over his head that seem to seal his fate in the eyes of those whom he depended upon to validate him in the past, setting off a domino effect of events. Standing yearly invitations to speak at former churches in the denomination were cancelled. Phone calls to trusted, dear friends and associates went unanswered. In addition, accidental crossing of paths with acquaintances resulted in awkward disingenuous banter and a sigh of relief when it was over. He had been ostracized and he knew it.

The family wisdom ran strongly against this decision. William's father called it "Ridiculous," with his certain and forceful stress on the second syllable, "RiDICulous," and his sisters, although cautiously silent, were concerned he was hasty, and a few questioned whether this could possibly ruin his future in ministry. Amidst the rising tide of turmoil, he too, for brief moments, quietly had his own doubts. Nevertheless, he moved forward with his plans trembling but trusting in something that was brewing within that was beyond his ability to deny or resist. He was face to face with what could easily be described as the perfect storm.

Confronted By His Reflection

William had flown to Atlanta, Georgia to attend a conference hosted by Azusa Fellowship International (a well-known non-denominational ministerial fellowship) that would become the ecclesiastical covering and ordaining entity for his ministry. He had just returned to his room at the Omni hotel downtown Atlanta from the evening service of the conference. After undressing, he sat down on his bed and peered out the full length window of his room. It was tall, square, with a slight smoke-colored tint and an iron façade balcony on the seventeenth floor, where there was a spectacular view of the downtown skyline.

The darkness of night fall displayed the brilliant lit city of Atlanta. But a closer look also revealed William's reflection. He sat there reminiscing over the words of the preacher that night. The preacher spoke about *dying to self.* "Who am I? Who would I be dying to? Oh my God," He thought to himself. William wasn't sure anymore. Then a flood of memories washed over him like a broken dam releasing the stirring waters contained behind it. Feeling empty while being overwhelmed with uncertainty, William stood up and walked towards his reflection in the window and began a dialogue with the man he thought he was—the man he thought he knew.

With his right arm outstretched and his finger pointing, he asked his reflection, "Is this how you want to be remembered? I watch you dying daily—vanquished, defeated by the one thing even you could not outmaneuver—your ever evolving past—memories collapsing over the other with no form, no structure, no sense; focusing only on crisis and questions you may never come to know the answer to. Going forward, he said, "I now understand that I will have to choose my memories carefully." There are simply too many—faded friendships, dissolved relationships, more memorabilia and keepsakes than you know what to do with; personal letters from international and state officials, pastors, civic leaders. Volumes of books, home movies, and collectibles hint to your personal tastes. Articles, certificates, and diplomas reflect the level of accomplishments in schools and institutions you proudly attended. Tearstained photographs of your children with unmistakable resemblances of you and their mother etched deep into every fiber of their being.

William stood still in his room trying not to disturb the reflection of himself. As he gazed into the eyes of his reflection, they seemed to tell a story. He resisted the urge to walk away from this moment, but he was compelled to listen because of all the things that were revealed to him that night. He emerged with a new sense of purpose. Tonight would be the night. He could feel it deep in the marrow of his bones, the ebb and flow of memories' tide, and there was nothing he can do about it. He was no longer content simply to watch it—to watch his future rush away from him, leaving him alone with the ghost of past disappointments and failures, not knowing—never knowing if there was a future for him in ministry.

Wrestling all night for a breakthrough like Jacob with the angel of God before daybreak, a weary William dropped to his knees to pray before climbing into bed to get a few hours of rest before the early morning seminar. As he ended his prayer, a peaceful presence filled his room separating his thoughts from reason and logic—his awareness from his person and his reflection in the window—and God spoke to his mind:

> "Are you dead to that person yet? Choose your memories wisely. I will make up for the years of spoil and devastation. I will do a quick work and you will be full of praise to your God, the God who has set you back on your heels in wonder."

William fell onto his bed shaking and weeping as God's voice faded into a faint whisper—then to no sound at all. As subtle as God's presence filled his room that night, He lifted and left William to himself. Unaware when he drifted asleep, William awoke shortly before his wake-up call. He slid out of bed and walked to the bathroom to take a shower. Passing the mirror he noticed a worshipful look on the face of his reflection. It was the reflection of an emancipated figure of the enslaved man from the night before breathing easier, eyelids flickering with anticipation as if he had walked through an opened door in a parallel universe of unlimited possibilities.

The image William had become accustom to, dominated him as a man. That image died a slow death over a three year period of time, and the man he was and the man he was purposed to become met that night. He has never since been the same. His image now would be defined by God's acceptance and development rather than man.

True success is only possible when you *"Run your own race"* with God—with patience

~The Apostle Paul

Part II

Understanding Life's Transitions

I die daily a thousand deaths,
Only to triumph life's illusory web.

These deaths within resurrect a new life,
The one tradition conceals, the one that
Precludes my awakening from the
Picture perfect dream.

Arising, I see ahead of me ...
I see forming that which is now
Possible ... happiness ...
A breath without pain ...
My due.
~ Preston Williams II

Chapter 6

DYING TO BE ME

A GOOD EXERCISE FOR learning about yourself is to try viewing yourself objectively through the eyes of others. Consider what your family, colleagues at work, peers, and even strangers think of you. Now here's an interesting question:

> To what extent do you live up to their expectations
> or to the image they have of you?

In an environment where everyone wants to be socially accepted, it is common that other people's expectations about us directly affect how we behave and the type of person we become in that sphere of influence. Many people in such environments automatically sense how others view them; and if they aren't secure in who they are, they begin exhibiting the expected behaviors. This is mostly true in relationships or in professional settings where acceptance is paramount.

In Chapter 5, we read the story of William's experience in Atlanta, Georgia with God and his struggles with self-identity. He needed to understand who he really was apart from the expectations of his religious affiliations; the family ministry legacy, and the name he attempted to live up to. He saw these expectations as critically important to the man and minister he was predestined to be. Like William, we all struggle with who we are versus who we should be. Transitioning to the person you should be requires dying to "old man nature"; or the "constructed self" you have come to know as "you."

The concept of "dying to self" is found throughout the New Testament. It expresses the true essence of the Christian life, in which, we take up our cross and follow Christ. Dying to self is part of being born again. The old self dies and the new self comes to life (John 3:3-7). But there is more, we also continue dying to self as part of the process of sanctification. As such, dying to self is both a one-time event and a lifelong process.

It is a lifelong process because according to God's word, "the heart is deceitful above all things, and desperately wicked: who can know it?" (KJV). The human heart (mind, emotions, and will) is more deceitful than anything else in God's universe. It is so desperately wicked that we cannot even know it; we cannot understand the dimensions of human depravity. Even many of the good acts (humanly speaking) that humans do are done unconsciously for sinful motives (for example, to impress others or to deceive ourselves into thinking we are basically good).

Moses wrote:

> *The Lord saw how great man's wickedness on the earth had become, and that every inclination of the thoughts of his heart was only evil all the time. The Lord was grieved that He had made man on the earth, and His heart was filled with pain.* (Genesis 6:5-6)[1]

To die to self is to set aside what we want in this moment and focus on what God's desire is for us. This moves us away from the "self" that is given to natural inclinations and closer to becoming the person of purpose God intended. It's much easier to deal with the concerns, needs and challenges that life throws at us when the person we're becoming is in line with the person God has preordained us to become and when we are to the place where His "will" consumes us.

Jesus described the dying-to-self process (to "deny self" is the exact scriptural phrase) as part of following Him:

> Dying to self is a part of the internal purging process—the Christian principle of sanctification.

> *If anyone wishes to come after Me, he must deny himself, and take up his cross and follow Me* (Matthew 16:24, NASB). Dying to self is not to be avoided nor seen as an egregious task. Actually, it should be celebrated as the rite of passage to discovering who you really are; it is the true *self* that is only revealed through process of dying to the pre-conversion *self*. Jesus continued: *Self-help is no help at all. Self-sacrifice is the way, my way, to finding yourself, your true self.* (Matthew 16:25, the Message Bible)

A few years ago, I was reading a wonderful book entitled, *Becoming a Vessel God Can Use.* The author, Donna Partow, expressed her concern for how people are obsessed over their external appearance—public image and not their internal image. She deals with this issue from a woman's perspective because of the extent women will go through to achieve a certain look or impress certain individuals.

Cosmetics and cosmetic surgery are multi-billion-dollar industries in America. So much of a woman's identity is caught up in how she looks. Imagine the desperation of a woman who would allow someone to slice open her breast and insert a plastic bag filled with chemicals, believing that somehow, someway, that will bring her the happiness and fulfillment she longs for. The fact of the matter is, it is a universal problem that affect both men and women.

Some Christian pastors and teachers have fallen for the same shallow quick fix mentality in the church environment. They help people look good on the outside, ironing out the wrinkles of selfishness, tucking in the fat of sin. We just want to look good on the outside of the vessel. Never mind the inward reality; we want bandages, we want quick fixes.

Partow further expressed that she was, fed up with "the secret keys," "the 22 ways," and "the surefire plan." I'm fed up with the phony masks of self-styled Christian experts and the dishonesty of those who proclaim one thing while living something completely different. The only reason the church is so disillusioned when these people fall, is because they followed after the persuasiveness of men, rather than looking for a demonstration of the Spirit's power.

With each passing day, I become more determined to know nothing except Christ and the power of His resurrection. I don't have all the answers. I haven't arrived. I don't have a perfect marriage or the perfect child. I only know that Jesus Christ has done something incredible in my life. I was lost and now I'm found. I was blind and now I see…it is not *nirvana.* But it is forward progress. And the only way I can explain how I got from where I started to where I am is… it was a God Thing.[2] It was my decision to accept God's plan for my life and the first order of business was to die to my "self" and allow God to do His thing in my life.

In dying to self, we find our authentic self by depending on God who provides much more than we can imagine. You can never receive what has been determined for you by God until you become who God has predetermined you to be and that requires dying to who you think you are. Likewise, Jesus taught in John 12:24:

> *Unless a grain of wheat falls into the ground and dies,*
> *it remains alone; but if it dies, it produces much grain.*
> (NKJV)

Man is under attack, Not only is man lost, incomplete, and depraved, but he is under constant attack by a most powerful enemy—Satan. Satan desires that nonbelievers stay in spiritual darkness (John 3:19-21). He also prowls about seeking to destroy the mental health of Christians (Ephesians 6:11-16; 1 Peter 5:8-9). There are various devices Satan uses to accomplish these purposes. He can deceive, enticing people to pay attention to false doctrines (1 Timothy 4:1-3). He can influence thinking, causing man to focus on his own interests rather than on God's (Matthew 16:21-23). Satan can hinder the spread of the gospel (1 Thessalonians 2:2, 14-16). Satan can tempt (1 Corinthians 7:5). He can oppress people mentally, even to the point of driving them insane (Luke 8:26-39).

But although demonic possession is possible, Satan usually chooses to work in far more subtle ways today. For example, he best accomplishes his purposes with Christians by tempting them over and over in the area of their greatest weakness, whether materialism, pride, lust, a tendency toward depression, or whatever. The great variety of Satan's schemes is then, another factor of which the Christian counselor should be constantly aware.[3]

With much caution I don't want you to mistake dying to self as the death of self. Self-denial is not self-rejection. God treasures your divinely created self. He doesn't want to obliterate the part of you that makes you uniquely you. God works within you and reshapes you into the person your renewed-in-Christ self is meant to be— unselfish with what you own, not envious when others seem to get what you want, and not anxious about how you will make it through tough times. When you understand the God of *how*, you shouldn't live in despair, certainly not forsaken, and absolutely not destroyed because you know that God has you covered.

The Apostle Paul wrote words of affirmation concerning this truth in his second letter to the church at Corinth (2 Corinthians 4:7-9). He said, "But we have this treasure in jars of clay to show that this all-surpassing power is from God and not from us. We are hard pressed on every side, but not crushed; perplexed, but not in despair; persecuted, but not abandoned; struck down, but not destroyed." (NIV)

So Exactly What Does Dying To "Self" Look Like

As we die to self, we no longer try to enforce our agenda or expect people to validate us. We saw William in Chapter 5 struggling with the image developed by not only an organization but also associates that he later became depended upon to affirm him. When we die to self, we let go of trying to impress others. Although people may be impressed, your intention will be to represent God by being the best "you" you can be for His glory. When we do, we will find freedom from the self-focused life.

I remember reading an article about Evelyn Underhill a few years ago. She said something that really stuck with me. As an English Anglo-Catholic writer and pacifist, she was known for her numerous works on religion and spiritual

> Satan desires that nonbelievers stay in spiritual darkness—he desires to keep them lost, incomplete, and depraved.

practice. She wrote that: "We mostly spend [our] lives conjugating three verbs: to want, to have and to do. Craving, clutching and fussing, we are kept in perpetual unrest." This statement spoke to me. I realized that an unregenerate self will always be in search for the next emotional and physical fix. But when we die to self, we're no longer obsessed with self-indulgence. Dying to self actually makes life easier because, for example, we can be content even when we're in the most turbulent storms of life while others all around us are being celebrated and doing well.

In 1999, I was in graduate school pursuing my Master degree in Theology. I had left pastoring in the suburbs to plant a church in the inner city of Riviera Beach, Florida. The church was birthed from a Bible study I was asked to teach at a men's rehabilitation center called J.A.Y. (Jesus and You) Ministries. If you know anything about Riviera Beach during that time you would quickly remember it being one of the most at-risk cities in Florida and among the highest in crime in the nation. With drug infested streets, robberies, prostitution, and constant gun fire which resulted in the loss of many lives, Riviera Beach was indeed a societal war zone.

At the invitation of the Director of the J.A.Y. Ministries, I taught empowerment lessons every Tuesday night for a few months. Eventually, I was asked to consider planting a church from among the many men and their families who had become transformed by the teaching. I did. Within a year I had to relocate the ministry to the John F. Kennedy Middle School band room. News spread of the newly organized ministry birthed from the regeneration center for men. A month and a half later we had outgrown the band room and had to move the services to the gymnasium of the middle school. It was an unmistakable move of God.

The annual banquet for the center was approaching, and I was invited to attend. It was well supported by city officials, businessmen, and even the celebrated actor Ben Vereen was in attendance. The banquet was held at the exclusive Governors Club in the Phillips Point building in downtown West Palm Beach, Florida. It was an amazing event to say the least. As the night progressed, men who had graduated from the rehabilitation program were asked to tell their story. It was a testimony to the impact and effectiveness of the program which would garner the financial and political support of the influential attendees.

One after the other they walked up to the podium and spoke of their life of crime and/or drug abuse and how they came to give their life to Christ. They spoke of the change that they experienced in their heart, with their families, and how they wanted to give back to their communities. Each spoke about the people who had influenced them. I thought they would mention my name, but they didn't. After a while, I considered excusing myself early. But it quickly occurred to me that I was experiencing a mentoring moment by God. Deep within, I knew the Spirit, not me, had done a great work in their life. In fact, the rehabilitation center was the place used to introduce these men to the God of *how*. He would not only set them free, but introduce them to who He created them to be. The reality was that God will work through anyone He chose to navigate them through the rest of their life experiences. It wasn't about me. I also saw this as an exercise in dying to self by not squeezing myself into the spotlight.

The questions I had to ask myself that night after I return home were valuable to my ministry growth. Could I honor others above myself? In Romans 12:10, Paul writes to the church at Roman, "Be devoted to one another in love. Honor one another above yourselves." (NIV) But this issue went even deeper:

> *Could I be secure in God's love without public recognition? Could I let God be in charge of my reputation? Was God's approval enough for me?*

After this early exercise in dying to self, I eventually found myself relying on God more in small things. I was finding my new life—the companionship and partnership with God that I longed for.

A New You—A Fresh Start

Life will always present more challenges for you to contend with. And more significant life lessons lie ahead. God will be right there to assist you through the process of how you might die to self a little each day. In our "me-first," materialistic culture, it might mean something as simple as refraining from a diet that maybe harmful to your health, or not becoming defensive when mocked, humiliated, or grilled about a questionable situation. As you work through the process of dying to self, discover how God will consistently meet your needs as you grow spiritually in your new life and find the authentic you.

These daily behind-the-scene processes train us to be selfless in small ways so that when we find ourselves in bigger struggles of faith, we more easily set aside our self-focused desires and think about God's intention for those ordained moments. If we truly seek to discover the life we were born to live within God's intention and ignite it with passion, we will begin to experience the abundant life Christ promised to us. In doing so, we also become good stewards of the dreams and visions (God's intentions for our life) assigned to us.

In a final note, we need to be able to make good choices if we want to be a good steward of not only our life and dreams, but also our own heart which will lead us in the right direction. Wise choices will watch over you. Proverbs 2:11 says:

> *Discretion will preserve you; understanding will keep you.* (NKJV)

Did you know that? If we desire to receive the fullness of the blessings of God so that we can be a greater blessing to others, we must make a commitment to invest the time and energy it takes to develop our true selves.

Maybe you're saying, "I want to do that, but how do I do that?" I am not talking about developing your talents and your gifts, although that is a good thing to do. But when you really desire to develop yourself, you need to put forth the effort to increase yourself on the inside so you can be on the outside that entire person God has called you to be. When we are born again, accepting Jesus as our Lord and Savior, we received certain spiritual gifts or abilities as a member of the Body of Christ. As we grow in a personal relationship with Christ, we will be well on our way to discovering the person that God created us to be.

Chapter 7

In The Toils of Change (Story)

Boynton Beach, Florida 1999

SIX YEARS HAS PASSED since William experienced his life changing visit to an Atlanta conference. He had enrolled into graduate school; he had planted an interdenominational church in the inner city of Riviera Beach, Florida, and he had weathered the storms of being ostracized because of divorce and major ministry changes. Some relationships were slowly on the mend—including his relationship with his father. Through all the brutal turmoil that seemed to smash him, one after the other—it appeared that God had his back after all.

Reflecting on the shadows and turns and surface of his life, he pictured a future with personal resolve. Time was passing. He was in a much better place emotionally and spiritually. On this particular day, William took the off day to spend with his parents. The night before, he was at home in his study in Boca Raton preparing for a seminar. He suddenly felt a deep dearth in his heart, a longing for his parents; thinking of his mother's sweet gentle heart, her soft toned voice, and her effervescent smile that would bring calm to any room she entered, and his father's light-hearted stories that he would tell of experiences in church that would have you gasping for breath from astonishment and disbelief or bending over with gut wrenching laughter–because the funniest things can and do happen in church. It brought back a few fond memories of the past fused into one intense flash of awareness. He needed to see them. Because of the demands of graduate school, travel, and his ministry, he had not seen his parents for almost a year. It occurred to William that the "tomorrows" with his parents would be few because they were getting older.

It had been almost fifteen years since William's parents retired from their secular careers, left St. Marys Georgia and relocated to Palm Beach County Florida to serve in full-time ministry. His father had been assigned as Senior Pastor of a large church in West Palm Beach Florida. While visiting their home in Boynton Beach, William moved through this once foreign house and had become accustomed to it as though this was the place he'd always come home to. His mother's touch filled each room with her unique class, silent charm, and motherly warmth. With her freshly planted shrubs and blossoming flowers in the front yard nicely arranged to her specifications, and her vegetable garden in the backyard, it was home—living again with nature and nurture.

Outside in the backyard, William joined in the routine Saturday morning yard work with his parents. They laughed and talked about different encounters during their week. Eventually, his mother worked her way toward the front yard and his father began mowing the lawn in the backyard. William picked up a hedge trimmer and began trimming along the north side of the house. The work tasks separated William from his parents for a few moments. As he continued to work, William thought of a statement he read recently in an article by Christiane Northrup, M.D.

Dr. Northrup was writing about the power of our history and how it influences us. He wrote, "To become optimally healthy and happy, each of us must get clear about the ways in which our mother's history both influence and continue to inform our state of health, our beliefs, and how we live our lives." William couldn't shake a recent conversation he had with his other siblings about how their mother was the cohesive glue that bonded the family together. They reminisced about the many Thanksgiving family gatherings that brought them together because of her.

Thanksgiving was indeed a time of laying aside any differences they may have had with each other and focusing on the importance of family. Whenever William thought of Thanksgiving, a convergence of emotions and traditions seem to trigger epiphanies about his parents. His mother would be in the kitchen with his five sisters making final dinner preparations before they all took their places at the table in the formal dining room. You could hear the playful sounds of his nieces and nephews in different parts of the house and outside the kitchen window. William and his brother, along with the brother-in-laws, would be in the family room with his father watching one of the "Holiday Bowl" football games on television and bantering among themselves.

At some point during the conversations of the day, William's father would always find ways to resurrect embarrassing childhood memories that caused William's stomach to churn the same way it churned when he heard those stories as a boy. His father would share those memories in gest, lightheartedly as families do as they walked down memory lane. But William still felt uneasy about hearing them because these memories represented very different experiences for him than they did for the others. William could not get beyond the unresolved offenses intertwined in what should have been laughable, lighthearted memories. Suspended between getting upset and letting it slide, William would find a way to be deeply thankful on those Thanksgiving holidays; at least he still had a father.

As William snapped out of his daydreaming state and finished up trimming the hedges, he made his way around to the front yard to help his parents gather the lawn equipment and tools. They carried everything to the storage room in the backyard and locked it down for the evening. As they made their way back to the house through the patio entrance, his father said, "The sun will be going down soon. I'd better turn the water sprinklers on before it get dark." William and his mother sat down on the patio to cool off while his father went to turn on the sprinkler system.

William began to talk to his mother about what brought him to the house that day. He began to express how he regretted not spending as much time with them as he would have liked. His mother just smiled as she always did and told William that she understood, having been in ministry with his father. She was quite aware of the demands of the ministry. William leaned over to his mother and said almost in a whisper, "I am really feeling regrets about not having the kind of close relationship with Dad that I know we could have had—and time is passing so quickly." William's mother listened as he continued to share his heart about the anger he felt as a child with his father and how it affected him as an adult—even now. William shared how he wanted to have a different relationship with his dad while he had time. But he was always bothered by some of his father's comments and actions that triggered bad memories of their past relationship.

Twenty or so minutes passed while William's father was still watering the lawn. It provided ample time for William and his mother to have some alone time together. William's mother allowed him to share his concerns and then she began to give William some motherly advice. Her words flowed with the calmness of care, yet, they had the counseling tone of biblical correction and wisdom. Listening to her rousing voice reinforced the urgency of William working more diligently on his part to form a father-son bond built on compassion and surrender.

William began to understand that he couldn't change his father. The only change he had the power to control was how he reacted to his father. He realized that he had to come to love his father in ways he had never loved him before. William knew that in order to do that, he had to unravel new layers of his father's character that were more likable and whimsical. Because of his mother's counsel, he embraced the fact that by learning to love his father differently, he would be free to become his strongest, truest self.

Night had fallen and William's father finished watering the yard and joined William and his mother on the patio. It was a quiet hot south Florida summer's night. William sat on his parents' screened patio looking at the shifting constellations of fireflies competing with stars as mosquitoes in flight slipped through an open door grabbing at the night air, and the sounds of their near-silent wings fluttered around his head. His parents talked a while longer with him, before walking back into the house. His mother busied herself cooking and washing a few dishes in the kitchen and his father eased himself into his designated recliner to watch his favorite evening TV game show. William leaned back on the patio lounger and turned his head to the side, quietly staring at his father through the slide-door that separated them.

Since that night in Atlanta, Georgia, William begun taking a hard look at the need to live urgently, as if each day were his last. He wanted to take swift action now to resolve or at the very least understand his relationship with his father; however, he knew that it would take the rest of his life. Now seeing himself as an adult, a father, and a minister, William was at that point in his life where he wanted to discover the lingering mysteries surrounding his dad, now a wisp of his former self and much calmer than he knew him to be. Though anxious, he would allow the answers to unfold one day at a time for the rest of his life.

He Is His Father's Son

He loved his father unconditionally now. Yet during a defiant adolescence and his early adult years, he sometimes felt that he hated him. His love for his father and his amazing mother was so deep now—at that very moment while sitting on the patio he was frighten that he almost discovered this level of love too late.

Grateful for the journey that brought him and his father to this place, and astonished by how God used turmoil, and personal change to move them from malice to reconciliation; he seized the moment. As the evening progressed, they were able to push through old anger and gingerly move from the pastor and bishop who happen to be his dad to the man who was now prepared to initiate the fatherly bond William had always desired.

Over the past few years, he struggled to reconcile many unsavory recollections with the few happy ones sprinkled in between, like precious stones, some as dark as black coal, others like luminous diamonds, and strung them into an expansive soul-searching circle of remembrance. The circle of remembrance contained sagas filled with more subtle annoyances that routinely came up between father and son, and scuffles that blurred the line of love.

The startling reality was that William's fantasy dad belonged to one of his friend, Alex Anderson. He resembled an actor from the Frank Sinatra and Sammy Davis Jr. days. He would speak to William with a big smile that seemed to diffuse whatever troubles William had whenever he visited with his son. Mr. Anderson would ask how William's parents were and place his hand on his head as if he was his own son. William never heard him shout.

Decades later, William found out that Alex's dad was divorced from his mom, lost the family home, was a wilted alcoholic whose son—his only son of five children, didn't speak to him. This demise happened while William's own iron-willed father had battled through a few personal issues, but he made it to retirement from the Gilman's Paper Company and relocated to Ft. Lauderdale, Florida to enter into the pastoral ministry full-time. His dad was still pastoring, still quick to slip in a critical word or two, still a refined connoisseur of men's suits, and he was still there married to his wife of almost fifty years at that time. There was a moral to William's childhood delusion. It is the same delusion that holds true for much of life. The grass is not greener on the other side. When the curtains are parted in the house down the street, your own imperfect father will look pretty good.

One thing William came to know beyond the turbulent history they shared was that he was his father's son, and he knew it because at that moment, God showed him how—through forgiveness and unconditional love. Believe it or not, he thanked God for the challenges that forced him to desire change and for the turmoil that followed. It was a difficult season in his life, one that represented a slow death to an unhealthy part of his life, and one that would prove to be an elongated second chance to smooth out the contention between him and his father and get his life and ministry on the right path. This was a pellucid look into William's father/son toils and reconciliation, a living breathing testament of God's use of his experiences to develop him forward.

Chapter 8

LEARN FROM YOUR PAST BUT LIVE FOR NOW: LIFE CHANGE

Change has a considerable psychological impact on the human mind.
*To the **fearful** it is threatening because it*
means that things may get worse.
*To the **hopeful** it is encouraging because things may get better.*
*To the **confident** it is inspiring because the*
challenge exists to make things better.
~ King Whitney Jr.

Can You Get to Your Future If Your Past is Present?

TIME WAITS FOR NO-ONE. Time will pass quickly or slowly depending on your vantage point. It will work for you or against you, depending on the decisions you make. When past experiences ride the wave of expiring time, they begin to infiltrate your present life. Their effects occasionally find ways to enter your dreams while you are asleep at night. They can effectually sprinkle their unproductive negative influences throughout the waking hours of your day. When this happens, it is likely that you are in the grip of living life in reverse;

which creates an inability to grasp the future squarely and move forward. There will come a time when you must cease being stuck in the past. If not, the past will define you and mark every step you take for the rest of your life.

There is such a thing as having an addiction to your past. Over the years, addiction has been described in many different ways—a moral weakness, a lack of willpower, an inability to face the world, a physical sickness, and spiritual illness. Nearly all human beings have a deep desire to feel happy and to find peace of mind and soul. At times in our lives, most of us find this wholeness of peace and beauty, but then it slips away, only to return at another time. When it leaves us, we feel sadness and even a slight sense of mourning. This is one of the natural cycles of life, and it's not a cycle we can control. Addiction can be viewed as an attempt to control these uncontrollable cycles.[1]

Living in the past becomes an addiction when we attempt to control the out-of-control and aimless searching for wholeness, happiness, and peace through digging through archives of the past to revisit a place when things were much simpler, an unresolved relationship (good or bad), or an experience that haunts you even in your adulthood. No matter what your reason maybe for lingering in the past it detaches you from your present and ultimately your future. It is one thing to learn from your past. It quite another thing to live in it.

> Addiction can be viewed as an attempt to control uncontrollable cycles of living in the past.

In Chapter 7, William was at a place where he needed closure to past events and issues that caused him to become stagnate. There were valuable lessons he learned from the past. But there were some things he needed to resolve and release. Even though he was making some forward movement, it seemed as if there was an invisible ceiling limiting his success, happiness, and peace of mind. He would find himself drained from filling his days and nights with ministry *things-to-do* lists—yet there was still a lack of fulfillment. He was, as they would say in the old days, "sick and tired of being sick and tired." Rehearsing the past over and over in your mind each day can afflict your mind and body to the point of despair. It can also produce spiritual and emotional fatigue.

Fatigue is a dangerous creation of the mind. It dominates the lives of those who are living without direction and dreams. It can cause you to lose heart before you begin to attempt something great.

I was recently watching the third game of 2013 NBA playoffs between the Miami Heat and the Chicago Bulls. After beating the Miami Heat in Miami with an impressive victory, the Chicago Bulls had home court advantage because the third and fourth game of the series would be played in Chicago. Unfortunately, the Bulls lost both home games to Miami. After the fourth game during an interview, one of the Chicago Bulls players was interviewed, and he said that prior to the game he walked into the locker room and there sat his teammates.

The room was filled with a somber mood after having lost two straight games. Tonight would be their last home game before going back to Miami. After a huge win in Miami, the Bulls were now at 1 win and 2 loses. The interviewer asked the player for Chicago what he sensed walking into the locker-room. His response was each player looked fatigued—they were mentally not prepared to face the Heat.

They had lost the night before and Miami was showing no sign of backing down. Needless to say, the obvious lack of mental confidence displayed in the locker-room translated into a loss on the basketball court that night. The Chicago newspaper headlines that following morning read, "Heat Lower Boom on Fatigued Bulls."

Now compare the fatigue you feel in a moment when you are involved in something that is not engaging (emotionally or purposefully), and then a split second later you're invited to engage in something that brings a sense of joy, pleasure, or sparks enlightenment. Immediately, the fatigue vanishes. Fatigue then must be looked upon as a mental creation. It acts as a mental crutch when you're performing a tedious task, revisiting stressful negative past experiences or past events, and forecasting the uncertainties of the future. When you consistently direct your mind to live in the present you will always have boundless energy.

In the Bible, we are given two affirmations that signal the frustration of dwelling in the past and the anxiety of the unknowns of the future. The Apostle Paul writes to the church at Philippi:

> *Not that I have already obtained this or am already perfect, but I press on to make it my own, because Christ Jesus has made me his own. Brothers, I do not consider that I have made it my own. **But one thing I do: forgetting what lies behind and straining forward to what lies ahead**.* (Philippians 3:12-13 ESV Bible)

But then Jesus shares this amazing proclamation:

> *25. **Therefore I tell you, do not be anxious about your life**, what you will eat or what you will drink, nor about your body, what you will put on. Is not life more than food, and the body more than clothing? 26. Look at the birds of the air: they neither sow nor reap nor gather into barns, and yet your heavenly Father feeds them. Are you not of more value than they? 27. And **which of you by being anxious can add a single hour to his span of life?** 28. And why are you anxious about clothing? Consider the lilies of the field, how they grow: they neither toil nor spin, 29. Yet I tell you, even Solomon in all his glory was not arrayed like one of these. 30. But if God so clothes the grass of the field, which today is alive and tomorrow is thrown into the oven, will he not much more clothe*

*you, O you of little faith? 31. Therefore do not be anxious, saying, 'What shall we eat?' or 'What shall we drink?' or 'What shall we wear?' 32. For the Gentiles seek after all these things, and our heavenly Father knows that you need them all. 33. But seek first the kingdom of God and his righteousness, and all these things will be added to you. 34. **Therefore do not be anxious about tomorrow**, for tomorrow will be anxious for itself. Sufficient for the day is its own trouble.* (Matthew 6:25-34 ESV Bible)

In between *forgetting what lies behind* and *not being anxious about tomorrow* lies *now*. Within the simple passages of these two authors is a profound truth that must take root and resonate within your spirit if you are to be successful in your future endeavors. God has been, and forever will be responsible for the *how* of our life challenges. His only expectation from us is that we have a right relationship with Him, be obedience to Him, and trust in Him. Everything else will unfold in our life according to His predetermined plan for us.

Deactivating Your Past and the Temptation of Your Future

Living for now is only possible when we *lay aside every weight, and the sin which so easily ensnares us, and let us run with endurance the race that is set before us* (Hebrews 12:1). Living for now is out of reach

> Fatigue is a dangerous creation of the mind that dominates the lives of those who are living without direction and dreams.

for many of us because we get weighed down with baggage full of old memories, regrets, and hurts that we drag with us through the years. And the sin, sadly, is that we allow the baggage from our past to keep us from reaching our goals, developing proper relationships, and hinder us when we try to move forward.

Looking back at life and dwelling there too long is not the only cause of the hindrances, depression, and a lack of fulfillment. It is equally important to not attempt to see too far into your future nor dwell on it too long. These are distractions that effect our success in life. "Taking no thought for tomorrow" echoes our resolute dependence upon God's purpose and plans for us. He knows the entire strategy for our life from the beginning to the end. He says:

> *For I know the plans I have for you. They are plans for your good, not to destroy you or bring evil to you. These plans are for a future full of hope and promise.*
> (Jeremiah 29:11—Author's paraphrase)

Although God meticulously designed each detail of the *big picture* of His creation, He has chosen to expose us to only slices of our future within it during certain seasons in our life. He will never give you the whole plan upfront. You must trust Him daily.

I know. It is difficult to readjust our mind to accept and obey God's process for unfolding His ideas for us. We have a tough enough time dealing with the realities of what is right in front of us yet alone the unknown plans of God. The human mind, inherently impatient, triggers emotional reactions when our ideas about how things should be collide with how things are. We sometimes torment ourselves about choices we've made, words we've spoken, and the paths not taken. Perhaps we dwell on the future, postponing our happiness with thoughts about what is missing or wrong in the present moment. This is enslavement of our own making. Remember the biblical affirmations above—this enslavement is not God's choice for us.

There is no doubt that we live in the age of distraction. Yet one of life's sharpest paradoxes is that your brightest future hinges on your ability to pay attention to the present. Life unfolds in the present. But so often, we let the present slip away, allowing time to rush past unobserved and unseized, and squandering the precious seconds of our lives as we worry about the future and ruminate about what's past. We're living in a world that contributes in a major way to mental fragmentation, breakdown, distraction, and inconsistency. We are always doing something. Unfortunately, like a rocking horse, we are making a lot of movement but going nowhere. We allow little time to practice the stillness and calm that connects us to the mind of God to hear His counsel and direction.

Focusing on the present moment also forces you to stop overthinking. Being present-minded takes away some of that negative life and self-evaluation and getting lost in your mind— and in the mind is where we make the evaluations of life that beat us up. Instead of getting stuck in your head and worrying, you can let yourself go. In Chapter 7, William seize the opportunity to change his relationship with his father and to begin living life in the moment. Time was passing, his parents were getting older and he wanted a different life for himself. He no longer wanted to be a slave to his past.

I preached a message in Ft. Lauderdale, Florida a several years ago entitled "Now Faith for Your Now Moments." I expressed in the sermon that living in the now relieves you of stress producing a peace that will pass all understanding, a joy unspeakable, and undeniable happiness. A few days later a parishioner asked, "Why does living in the moment make people peaceful, joyful, and happier? Is it because, at that moment, they're basking in an overwhelming need being met? Will it not last? I looked in his eyes, and I said: the reality is that most negative thoughts concern either the past or the future.

Mark Twain had something to say about how we should view our future. He said, "I have known a great many troubles, but most of them never happened." Williams Shakespeare said, "Our doubts are traitors, and make us lose the good we often might win, by fearing to attempt." The hallmark of depression and anxiety is catastrophizing—worrying about something that hasn't happened yet and might not happen at all. Worry, by its very nature, means thinking about the future—and if you hoist yourself into awareness of the present moment—the now, worrying melts away. By releasing the bondage of yesterday and the anxiety of the future you can live a full productive life day by day.

I remember waking up the next morning after I had determined to resolve the issues that hindered my life. I knew I needed to map out a plan to free myself of unhealthy, daily worries and to be able to find a way back into the world again—a world I had always felt deprived of having. I knew that I needed to learn to live day to day with a new attitude and a clear progressive focus. I went about this by mapping out a plan to reclaim my life and myself. I decided I would make a list each night of exactly what I would accomplish the next day. I would not make the list too long. I wanted the list to be challenging but not so tedious that it would tempt me to abort my plan prematurely.

We Are Challenged but Not Changed

> Be present—focusing on the present moment forces you to stop worrying about your past and overthinking your future.

I have learned through my own life transformation that one of the most difficult things about the changes we need to make is not so much the challenge of change but rather the process of change. One of my favorite authors is Vance Havner. I believe the most profound words he has ever written was the following indictment against the modern day Christian. He said, "We are challenged these days but not changed, we are convicted but not converted, we hear the Word and do nothing with it, thereby we deceive ourselves." The hardest times for me in my season of change was when there was negative external pressure concerning decisions I knew were necessary. I was getting calls from opposing ministry officials, and people were predicting my demise. Amidst these challenges, I maintained my passion for change and for a relative ministry that would win my generation and influence the next. I wanted to know God's agenda for my life more than I wanted air to breathe. I kept a strong belief in my renewed self, and I listened to the excellent counsel and feedback from accomplished objective pastors and leaders.

Key Points of Change

Here are a few key points that have served me well during those times of change and have been invaluable throughout the years that would follow from one season of change to the next. As you begin the process consider the following:

- Is the change by choice or forced? You have more of a sense of peace and control if it is your choice. Submission to God's process is key.
- Examine your options. God will always provide a way out or a resolution.
- Make a list of resources and support. When your desires connect with God's plans and purposes, He will obligate Himself to bring you into the knowledge of things you need to know and also into the company of the people you need to know that is critical for your success.
- Use your support system. There are no lone-rangers in God's initiative in this world. Every person that God intersects with your life holds a valuable key to your "now" moment and will ultimately prove beneficial to the process.
- Maintain confidence in yourself and faith in God's track record of historical models and their end results.
- Know that each change has an ending, middle and new beginning. Notice I started with *ending*. This is where we all find ourselves right before the decision to change. It is a place of conclusion and resolution. The *middle* is the place of process and the *new beginning* is when you are totally invested and living out the desired change.

- You will feel overwhelmed at times, it is normal. Change comes at a price. Stress and tension is a part of that price. Like an aircraft uses stress and tension to take off and to gain altitude before it can get to cruise speed, we too need stress and tension. If properly dealt with, they could be used by God to propel us to the heights of strong character, personal fulfillment, and good success.

Lastly, just in case through the toils of dealing with your past or the anxiety of anticipating your future, you may have lost your ability to laugh, figure out a way for humor to be reintroduced in your life. According to King Solomon, laughter can certainly have healing powers: *"A merry heart does good, like medicine, but a broken spirit dries the bones."* (Proverbs 17:22-23 NKJV)

Laugh. Laugh daily and live.

Chapter 9

AND STILL I RISE (STORY)

Jacksonville, Florida—2002

IT WAS A CHILLY morning in late October, and William was taking a stroll on the Riverwalk along the north bank of the St. Johns River. The Riverwalks and St. John's River are valuable and beautiful gems for Jacksonville. Lining the north and south banks of the St. John's River, they are among the finest and most scenic in the state and a great place to spend an afternoon.

Growing up in the small town of St. Marys in southeast Georgia, Jacksonville was where William got his first exposure to the metropolitan lifestyle of a large city. His hometown was only thirty-five miles north of Jacksonville just across the Georgia/Florida state line. The last church his parents pastored was in Jacksonville before they retired and relocated to Palm Beach County, Florida. Jacksonville was where William finished high school because of the turbulence between him and his father during his early years in St. Marys, Georgia.

After years of traveling and at times relocating to various states for ministry training, planting churches, and pastoring, William finds himself back in this amazingly beautiful city where his young adult life began. With his cold fingers laced around the guardrails that line the Riverwalk, William was unable to lose himself in this luscious scene because mornings, unfailingly made him think of his mother who passed away two years earlier from pancreatic cancer. She was an early riser like him, and he knew if she was still alive she would be preparing breakfast for his dad who probably had already finished his first cup of coffee.

William recalled the final Thanksgiving dinner the family shared with his mother—it was at his parent's home in Boynton Beach, Florida autumn of 1999. Their relationship was solid; there had never been any rifts between the two of them. Yet, if he had known that he was spending their last Thanksgiving dinner together, he would have thanked her a thousand times for her unrelenting love, support, and nurturing influence as he wedged his face into the crook of her neck—his comfort spot as a child.

Now in his quiet times, when he is alone with her in his memories, William tells her all of the new things now that he never got to tell her, and hopes she is listening and still feels her son's love. He vows to her that he will not make the same mistake with his newfound relationship with his father, whom he never loved as much as he did his mother.

So much has transpired since her death. William finished graduate school with a Master of Arts degree in theology and went on to complete a Ph.D. in psychology and Christian counseling. It seems her life was sustained long enough just to witness the reconciliation of William and his father. It was as if she knew William needed this healing in his life in order for him to rise above all of the challenges he faced earlier on. It was she who taught him that letting go comes a lot easier when you are old enough to comprehend that fathers become the fathers that they are because of the fathers they had, or did not have. In other words, William's father was emulating the father that he grew up with.

William's healing could not have happened when he was younger. His innate craving for the father-care he never received from his dad—adoration, affirmation, and the male-bonding-strokes he had seen his childhood friend receive from his father was always a lingering hope. Like a thirsty man in a desert longing to drink from the mirage of an oasis that doesn't exist, William's adolescence was spent unfulfilled emotionally as a son—drinking from the illusion, but thirsty still. Because of his mother's love and counsel throughout the years, William, at the age of forty-three, finally understood who his father was and who he was not.

It's Time to Move Forward

During his visits to Jacksonville, William loved the ritual of morning espresso at Starbucks overlooking the busy downtown district before he began his day of meetings at Xavier University. No matter where he found himself on his travels, this perhaps was his most enjoyable tradition—sipping his espresso macchiato (all foam no milk) at 7 a.m. He was both effusive and expectant about the virgin day. It was too soon to have stressful thoughts. The air between his cup and his lips was fresh and clear and he had no idea that today would be a very important day, one that will change the course of his life.

A few hours later that morning, William met other ministers who were from different cities around the United States who were attending a conference in Jacksonville with an international fellowship of churches and ministers. Their presiding bishop had given a moving and thought-provoking commencement address at his college graduation a few years ago. Williams had the opportunity to meet the bishop after his graduation exercises and was invited to be a part of the international fellowship that the bishop was birthing.

At the time of their meeting, William was just coming through what he considered the perfect storm. After parting ways with his childhood religious denomination and the domino effect it had on his family and his life, he wasn't in a hurry to involve himself with another religious organization. William believed in accountability in ministry, but he had not found an institution that represented his beliefs, progressive ministry focus, and forward thinking that would provide a nurturing ecclesiastical covering. Two years had passed and although the bishop had given William the information concerning his church and the contact person for joining the fellowship, there was no contact.

Was it a coincidence that William was in town for a meeting on the same day of the conference the bishop planned two years earlier? I don't think so. William took the water taxi back to the Hilton Hotel where he was staying. As he walked through the hotel entrance toward the concierge's desk to complete his early check-in, he was met by none other than the bishop. William was greeted by the bishop with a strong handshake and his iconic big smile that appeared to light up the lobby of the hotel.

It was as if no time had pass since the bishop and William spoke at the graduation in August of 2000. His name was Bishop V.M. Potter. He was reverently yet simply referred to as "Bishop." Bishop Potter appeared to be intentional about their meeting in the lobby and a few seconds later William's intuition would prove to be true. Bishop Potter asked William if he could address the conference of ministers and pastors in the early session. William asked when the session would begin. Bishop Potter paused for a second or two and then he said, "You have fifteen minutes". William had a meeting at the University in two hours. William, in shock, thought to himself, "He must be kidding, fifteen minutes?!" But Bishop Potter wasn't kidding. This was very real and it was happening now! This was no small event and certainly not menial request. In order for one to grasp the magnitude of this moment, one would need to know who this man was.

Bishop V.M. Potter was founder and senior pastor of one of Jacksonville's most thriving mega churches. He hosted a worldwide religious broadcasting network, the founder and CEO of the famed Plaza Mall, and was the presiding bishop of over 100 ministries and pastors around the globe. It was a perfect, providential alignment of a reborn minister and his ministry coming into the reality of his spiritual father.

William was astonished at his own calmness. The impromptu invitation to speak at the conference by this stalwart man of God was overwhelming. Yet, there was an amused relief, like when in the midst of worry, one discovers there is no need for concern because you know that the God of *how* was in control of the moment. The feeling grew until it engulfed every part of his being.

William hurried up to his room and unpacked his computer, his bible, and the suit he planned to wear to the university. He sat down with only a few minutes to ponder what to say to this conference full of pastors, leaders, and ministers from around the country. No sooner than he entertained the question, this topic can to his mind, "The Past is the Past—Make Room for More." William was uncertain how this thought which became the topic of his message would be relative to the session that morning.

Within five minutes, William got dressed grabbed his Bible and exited his room. He entered the elevator and said a short prayer of assistance and gratitude for the opportunity to not only be at the conference but also to be a speaker in the conference. It would be the first time William ministered at this level since resigning his ministry from the denomination he grew up in.

As William exited the elevator and entered the ball room where the morning session of the conference was held, Bishop Potter had already alerted one of his staff to welcome him. William was identified and escorted to the reserved seating on the front row where other guest speakers were seated. It seemed to be the quintessential experience of the meaning of words and phrases that punctuate God's affirmation to those who are obedient to His desire and direction— like *favor* and *good success*. Two particular familiar scriptures seem to wash over William as he embraced the moment:

> *What then shall we say to these things? If God is for us, who can be against us,* (Romans 8:31 NKJV) likewise, *But we have this treasure in jars of clay, to show that the surpassing power belongs to God and not*

> *to us. We are afflicted in every way, but not crushed;*
> *perplexed, but not driven to despair; persecuted, but*
> *not forsaken; struck down, but not destroyed...* (2
> Corinthians 4:7-9 ESV)

In essence, under normal worldly and religious legalistic circumstances, William's odds of recovering his ministry were stacked against him. But God, in His strategic wisdom, process, and timing raised William above the fray of life; positioning him for Chapter 2 of his life and ministry. William addressed the conference that morning with humility, poise and a powerful message that drew thunderous applauses, constant amen(s), and concluded his message with the entire audience standing to their feet. As he collected his Bible to return to his seat, Bishop Potter embraced William and took the microphone in his hand and looking into his eyes. Bishop said, "Son," and with a brief pause he said again, "son, I now know why God intersected our lives. I know why He has brought us together. This is your time. This is your season and we have all been blessed in this conference by the insight God has graced you with to interpret His word and present biblical truth with such power."

Afterwards, the Bishop invited William to become a member of the fellowship and he became William's spiritual father. A few months later, after going through the licensing process of the international fellowship, William would be conferred with the highest license that can be obtained by a minister in the international fellowship—the Ordained Minister Certification.

A Time to Keep Silent, And a Time to Speak

The experience that morning left William in awe. When he drove in from Boca Raton earlier that morning, he never expected to see Bishop Potter; yet alone be involved in a major conference during his visit to Jacksonville. He was only there to attend a meeting for select alumni and board members at Xavier University.

Later that afternoon, William met with the university executives, and a few ministerial associates that served on boards of the university, but he was still fixated on the phenomenal experience at the conference. He was reluctant to share his experience with fellow associates at the meeting. They knew his downfall and recovery from being ostracized from his previous denomination and ministry leaders within the denomination who didn't take too kindly when he resigned his ministry with them.

Because William was such a private person, they were unaware of the depth of the transformation he had gone through over the past few years. The reconciliation with his father was a huge benchmark that facilitated healing from his past and from the effects of distancing his ministry from the denomination. With all of the personal changes unknown to them since his healing from past disappointments, he suspected they would frame his new outlook and decision to affiliate with a non-denominational fellowship in religious terms. This would translate into suspicion under the guise of spiritual discernment, and that would mean a discussion he preferred not having at that moment. Besides, if you discover you've suddenly crossed over into another chapter of your life that caught you by surprise, there is no sense in broadcasting it!

At that point, all William could think of was the story of Joseph the dreamer in the book of Genesis and how he shared the dream of influence and promotion in life given to him by God. His brothers became envious desiring to kill him and his dream. His father, Jacob, scrutinized the dream, but he never nurtured it. And although Joseph's rollercoaster ride of hardships and small-step successes resulted in the fulfillment of God's ultimate plan, William surmised that even in Joseph's story the lack of understanding of what God wants to accomplish will always be filtered first through the carnal mindset.

Robert E. Fisher in his book, *Quick to Listen Slow to Speak*, made an interesting observation through a quote that William remembered. Fisher said:

> "We may feel good about our words, our intentions, and our motivation may be pure but our message probably will be lost or misunderstood if we overlook how others are going to perceive what we say."

So William blended into the ranks of those who were attending the meeting and conjured up the wherewithal to be present at the meeting mentally and emotionally. But deep down on the inside, he was on another level spiritually. Like Joseph, William had been thrown into a proverbial pit by his brothers in ministry, cast into the prison of his mind to become enslaved by his past. But still, by God's grace and His ultimate purpose in William's life, he found himself with the wind of the Divine beneath him—lifting the wings of his ministry to rise and pursue his purpose once more.

In time, what God was doing through William, would need no specific voice nor explanation. It would just manifest. William knew just as the new life in the Spirit is conceived in the secret place of the soul, hidden from human eyes, likewise the birth of his renewed ministry and refocused life was also conceived in the secret place of his soul. His labor pains of suffering and the delivery of his new life was hidden from human eyes except for those who were privy to the process. William, even to this day, is in awe of the wonder and mystery of God's ways of revitalizing and fulfilling His plans and purpose in the lives of men and women. How God orchestrates the most unredeemable and dreary circumstances for our benefit and for His ultimate glory will always be a mystery.

For William, all he knew was that the wind of the Spirit blows where God wills it, and our souls hear the sound. We eventually see the evidences; however, we know not how this mysterious breath of God touches our human hearts and change the situations that will alter our life for the better.

Chapter 10

PREPARING FOR YOUR PROPHETIC NEW

WHY IS IT THAT everybody gets so excited at the beginning of a new year? Simply stated, people love the idea of renewal. They recite the familiar mantra in their mind, "out with the old, in with the new." It is very appealing for several reasons. If the previous year has felt stressful or tedious, then the prospect of a new beginning carries the feeling of renewed hope and possibility.

People have needs that only faith in God can meet. Through faith God assist us in dealing with the mysteries, the enigmas, and the tragedies of life. Mysteries are those imponderables such as worry over the origins of the universe and the meaning of life. Enigmas are those life experiences in which goodness does not always win and fairness does not always succeed. Tragedies are those events where the fabric of life is torn apart by death, by evil, and by accidents.[1] The God of *how* has answers to all of these.

If you are reading this book, there is a very good chance that you are in the valley of decision and life may not be working according to the way you have planned and you're looking for something fresh, a new direction. Perhaps, you're at the lowest point of your life. You're dead broke, in a less than ideal relationship, you're always under stress, and your life is full of chaos and clutter. It could be that you are always having to deal with emergencies and drama. You see no way out. Every time you try to do something to change your life for the better something bad happens and you wind up back in the same place. This is you, right? If not, keep living, you will get there. Everyone has an appointment with this season in their life. No-one is exempted from these experiences.

Psychoanalyst Erik Erikson proposed an understanding of the major need persons have at this time in their lives which relates well to the reassurance the God of *how* has to offer. According to Erikson, life is composed of a set of *ego-crisis* which people face at different stages of their lives. Those who are satisfied with the way they have lived their lives and would live them over again in the same manner will have the healthiest egos. Their sense of life's integrity will provide them the inner strength to face life as they get older. Despair is the lot of those whose reflections cause them to feel that their lives have had little worth. They are deeply frustrated that they have no chance to live life over in a different way.

The Christian tradition meets this need to avoid despair and to affirm integrity. Its message is one of not only judgment, but grace, confrontation and comfort. It preaches both that God will provide, and it challenges that we are to believe that life is not over.[2]

> Through faith and patience, God guides us through the mysteries, enigmas, and tragedies of life.

If you desire change, you must decide to do it now. Tomorrow is always the ideal time for the procrastinator; consequently, tomorrow never come. You must also be willing to never look back! You need to be ready to put your old life behind you! If this is where you are then keep reading. No one can make you want to change your life, but you. No one! When your prophetic "new" is upon you, you will need to make some major adjustments between your ears. You need to think like a new person, act like a new person, dress like a new person, surround yourself with new people. You will need to start thinking positively. Put away the, *I can't*, *what ifs*, and *maybes* and get down to the nuts and bolts of changing your life.

In Chapter 9 William was experiencing a renewal of his life and the continuing transformation of his spirit. William later realized the he was entering into his prophetic new—that point in his life initiated by God based on a word He spoke into his life in the past that is now coming into fruition. In Chapter 3, William was a teenager who had an unusual encounter with God. It was his call to ministry, and it came with a promise that was unfolding twenty-seven years later.

He was stepping out of what represented the old and stepping up into a new level of possibilities. God was with him just as He promised William the summer of 1975. William had transitioned out of several years of personal and professional bondage and eagerly embraced the idea of making positive forward changes in his life. He allowed God to open his eyes to transforming principles from His Word. And he postured himself to walk fearlessly on the prophetic new path God was orchestrating.

William's renewed confidence in his fresh outlook for the future didn't come without a price. He had to conquer some potentially lethal adversaries for his happiness and success to come into fruition such as: bitterness, rejection, isolation, and fear. The worst of the four was fear. When dealing with a fresh start in life, the fear we feel is usually connected to the assumption that we can't succeed without starting life all over again. This is because our old nature wants us to believe that the path to a new life requires retracing our steps and fighting our way back to an unsoiled starting place in life. Just thinking about it can be tedious and tiresome. But here's the good news, the truth is that the secret place of all fresh starts in life unfolds right from where we are in each moment that we will dare to leave who we have been behind us.

In this prophetic new life, there are a few new adjustments that will be critical for you to deal with up front. You must have a right relationship with God and man. Your right relationship with God will make your relationships with man easier to bare and to manage. Concerning your relationships with man, if there are any fractured associations that can be repaired they should be repaired and begin afresh like it is the first time. Relationships that cannot be repaired should be forgiven and released. Now here is a challenging adjustment; every discouragement must be properly resolved in your spirit, and considered *over* right now. Every challenge, every difficulty should be shouldered only in its time and should never be carried forward or looked back upon with regret. Your prophetic new life is predicated on your commitment to making these basic adjustments that should be made now.

> "Start by doing what's necessary; then do what's possible; and suddenly you are doing the impossible."
> ~St. Francis of Assisi

> Bitterness, rejection, isolation, and fear are lethal adversaries to happiness and success. The worst of the four is fear.

The prophetic new life is not something that can be accomplished by an event, a trip, a conference, or even an incredible moment of revelation. There are no quick fixes. There is no oil sold in either the Christian bookstores or grocery stores that can be prayed over and pour over you that can bring it to pass. It is a God ordained process, and there is no getting around it. You've got to do what is necessary; it is the hallmark of achieving the "new" in your life.

New is a God Idea

Really! New is a God idea. If you doubt me, let's take an historical look back at God's relationship with the children of Israel. There are two words that punctuate His prophesy concerning their future. The words are: *now* and *new*. Isaiah wrote:

> But **now** *thus says the Lord, he who created you, O Jacob, he who formed you, O Israel:* "Fear not, for I have redeemed you; I have called you by name, you are mine. When you pass through the waters, I will be with you; and through the rivers, they shall not overwhelm you; when you walk through fire you shall not be burned, and the flame shall not consume you." (Isaiah 43:1-2)

Through Isaiah's writing God continues to prophesy over the children of Israel saying:

"Remember not the former things, nor consider the things of old. 19. Behold, I am doing a **new** thing; **now** it springs forth, do you not perceive it?" (Isaiah 43:18)

God is fascinated by new things. In the Book of Genesis, we see Him in all of His creative splendor. In the beginning God created. What did He create? The obvious answer would be heaven and earth. But a more insightful eye would notice first and far most that God created something *new* from *nothing*. There was no evidence before Genesis that heaven and earth existed. His creation was to be progressive and ever-evolving.

Even when Lucifer fell from the presence of God because of rebellion and caused a perfect creation to turn into chaos and darkness, God didn't allow Lucifer's disruption and failure to hold creation hostage. He began another cycle of *new*. God saw the distortion of His original creative master-plan and He spoke these words of restoration: "Let there be." All that was needed was His spoken Word and progressive order was reestablished.

That same spoken word reestablishes dashed dream that were sifted from us because of bad choices. It is the same scrutinizing eyes of God that desires His master-plans to not be held hostage. He has promised us:

> *The steps of a good man are ordered by the Lord, and*
> *He delights in his way. Though he fall, he shall not be*
> *utterly cast down; For the Lord upholds him in His*
> *hand.* (Psalms 37:23-24)

This is a provisional promise for those stuck in a distorted way of life. And though it is easy to fall into the *woe is me* mentality, there is always a part of us that know that we were meant for something better. Depression begin its onset and eventually takeover when we are unable to access the "better" that we can't just quite put our finger on, or the "new" that is so amazing it seems to escape the possibility that we are the intended recipient.

We were thoughtfully and intentionally created in God's image. Our image was decided on behind closed doors in heaven by the unanimous vote of the Triune Godhead who said, "Let us make man in our image and after our likeness" (Genesis 1: 26a). Because we are created in the image of God, like Him, we inherently possess the desire to have new experiences, new opportunities, and the need to create them if they do not exist. One of the many paradoxes of human creativity is that it seems to benefit from constraints. Although we consider imagination as requiring total freedom, the reality of the creative process is that it is often entangled with strict bonds and formal necessities. Most songs have choruses and refrains; symphonies have four movements; plays have five acts, etc.

Daily life is full of these creative constraints. We refer to them at times as obstacles, such as: a construction site blocking the usual road to work, a colleague's back-biting interfering with one's chances of a promotion, a newborn child postponing a parent's desire to find a job or perhaps finish college, or a lack of resources standing in the way of realizing an ambitious plan. How do we cognitively respond to such obstacles? How do the ways in which we perceive and process an experience change when an obstacle interferes with what we want to accomplish? I suggest that unless we are inclined to disengage prematurely from ongoing activities, obstacles will always co-exist with daily life.

The prophetic new life requires that we use these constraints, or obstacles if you prefer, to prompt us to step back and adopt a more global

> Discomfort, if properly understood, can often provoke insight

perspective that permits us to look at the *big picture*. Obstacles, more than not, often cause us to walk the tightrope of discomfort, and discomfort, if not properly understood, will cause us to enter into an unhealthy state of brokenness. If we lean too far in one direction then we view all human discomfort as problematic. Discomfort, if properly understood, often motivates insight. When we attempt to prematurely abandon or ignore the process of God through these experiences, we short-circuit their opportunities for emotional and spiritual growth.[3]

Constraints, discomforts, obstacles, and pain are components of our fallen nature. But a healthy awareness of human fallenness will enhance our relationship with God by getting our eyes off ourselves and onto God's magnificent character.[4]

And even if we can't see what God sees, through faith and patience, we allow God to create something new despite our experiences (good, bad, or indifferent). What I found that is so amazing is that God has the ability to integrate seemingly unrelated pieces of our life into a purposeful new direction if we will just trust Him.

The Cycle of Your Prophetic New

The cycle of God's prophetic *new* begins when your imagination, intention, creation, perception, and experiences fail—over and over again. It is when your failure results in your desires aligning with God's will. At that time, God reveals His predetermined intention and a new door opens. Being aware that God is unique and no one can change His mind concerning His plans for us, and that He performs what He has predetermined for us (Job 23:13-14), we should wait on Him in the background of life. We should be totally passionate about our personal talents, spiritual gifts, and assignment in this world. Appreciatively watching and waiting for the opened door God will orchestrate on our behalf in His own timing, once revealed, we should promptly execute the plan by faith—unwavering, with all boldness.

In the scriptures at the beginning of this chapter, we see the historical account of God proclaiming a new thing in Israel's state of despair. God was ending Israel's cycle of wandering in their proverbial wilderness of bondage and failure. They were guilty of doing things their way, and now we find them at a place where they had no other choice but to hear God. What God was saying to Israel, in our modern terms, was: "Where I am taking you is not like where you have been before; I want to introduce you to something new. It is nothing like I've delivered you from before; this will be another dimension of new." But Israel needed a fresh anointing or an infusion of God's divine influence which results in a renewed spirit. God was announcing a shift that would make Israel a prosperous nation, an empowered culture, and a military force to be reckoned with. But Israel needed a redemptive revelation. They needed to change their focus from what was "former" to what is "now," and from what was "old" to the new direction God was prophetically espousing for them.

The last four chapters, I dealt extensively with the dangers of holding on to the past. Israel was challenged to release the past and refocus on the next new adventures with God. You too must refocus. Where God is taking you your past has no reference points to efficiently guide you because it is new. You need a brave new spirit to trust God in order to receive the new direction and the new promises that God has lined up to release into your life.

Another one of Israel's historical mentoring moments points to Joshua after the death of Moses. Before Joshua could successfully lead and conquer the city of Jericho and ultimately the Promised Land, he needed an authentic new attitude and an unpretentious new public persona. Joshua was challenged by God to, "Be strong and of good courage, do not fear" (Joshua 1:5-7 NKJV). God issued Joshua the promise of prosperity and success with a repetitive condition: "Only be strong and of good courage and do not be afraid. And observe to do according to all in the Book of the Law." God spoke the promise and the conditions three times. I think, He was drilling the key to success into Joshua's mental consciousness to nurture and renew his spirit. I can imagine God saying to Joshua, "Perhaps that went over your head. Let me reiterate it, don't miss it!"

Success is guaranteed if you listen when the Lord speaks, heed His direction, personify bravery, and operate in the right/renewed spirit. Spiritual renewal in hard times is essential for emotional and personal well-being during our spiritual journey. All around us each day, we are faced with the negative side of life staring us in the face. Gas prices and a failing economy take us prisoner, devastating weather conditions threaten lives and lifestyle, even television and movies inundate us with depravity and negativity.

Consequently, what we place our attention on becomes our focus and our focus translates into who we become. Therefore, spiritual renewal is absolutely necessary today for survival. As Christians, we must get back to craving biblical truth—the fountain of living waters. Without the discipline of renewing the mind, Christians will not be mentally prepared to receive directives and assignments from God. If believers' minds are filled with deceitful, sensual and worldly thoughts, God cannot entrust them with His plans and purpose. The Word of God is urgently needed in these times. God's people need to rise up, first in disciplined thinking, then in a disciplined lifestyle. This is critical. It forms the basis for us to know Him, to adore Him and to obey Him.

Thinking God's Way

I remember when I was a child growing up in my parents' home. During frustrating moments, when I would do something weird like most kids, my sweet mother would say in a stern voice, "For God's sake, use your head for more than a hat rack!" Although it was a bitter-sweet reprimand, I came to understand that she valued my mind. She knew I was capable of thinking on a higher level than what I was using my mind for at the time.

As a creature made in God's image, we have been gifted with a mind, heart, and soul. God expects us to function through a balanced use of these gifts. We can walk in confidence knowing that the Lord will guide and shape the gift of human thinking, bringing us ever more fully into the light.

To hear God speak through both human and divine wisdom means to learn how to properly "Think in the Spirit." You must assume an active, yet yielded position before God. The desire to grasp the wisdom that God offers to us is crucial to our progressive development and key to possessing all that God have predetermined for us.

Timothy, the sidekick and favorite spiritual son of the Apostle Paul, gives us an exhortation in the critical role the Word of God plays in the life of the believer:

> *Every part of Scripture is God-breathed and useful one way or another—showing us truth, exposing our rebellion, correcting our mistakes, training us to live God's way. Through the Word we are put together and*

shaped up for the tasks God has for us. as 2 Timothy 3:16-17 teaches (The Message Bible).

The best way to learn the will of God is simply by reading His Word. After Moses died, Joshua was ordained to lead God's people into the Promised Land. God told Joshua:

> *This Book of the Law shall not depart from your mouth, but you shall meditate in it day and night, that you may observe to do according to all that is written in it. For then you will make your way prosperous, and then you will have good success.* (Joshua 1:8 KJV)

To meditate means to consider deeply, or think about intently and at length. This will mean not only reading, but studying, and memorizing verses of scripture, and thinking about

> **Success is guaranteed if you: listen when the Lord speaks, heed His direction, personify bravery, and operate in the right spirit.**

their meaning and personal application. This process refreshes the spirit of man. It stimulates confidence in the face of the unknown and keep us moving forward.

David, the King of Israel, contributed his personal success to basking in God's Word. He said, "Your word I have hidden in my heart, that I might not sin against You" (Psalm 119:11). David also understood the value of a brave new spirit when in pursuit of your dreams and achieving the purpose of God. One of David's many prayers included a *critical* component that make any of our petitions to God worthy of His attention. He simply said: "Create in me a clean heart, O God; and renew a right spirit within me" (Psalms 51:10). Knowing the debilitating influence of our sinful nature, David acknowledged his need for God to change him inside out. His success depended upon it.

Guard Your Thought Life

We are spiritually victorious or defeated moment by moment, and day by day, in proportion to the thoughts we think. What we feed our minds and dwell on has a tremendous impact on whether we will be victors or victims. Ephesians 4:23 states "Be renewed in the spirit of your mind." Colossians 3:10 teaches us to: "Put on the new man who is renewed in knowledge." The spiritual gift inside is God-given, holy, and perfect. As Christians we lack nothing spiritually. However, God never oversteps our freedom of will. God does not control our minds. It is the Christian's responsibility to change the way he thinks!

M. Scott Peck, an American psychiatrist and author, once wrote, "The whole course of human history may depend on a change of heart in one solitary and even humble individual; for it is in the solitary mind and soul of the individual that the battle between good and evil is waged and ultimately won or lost."[5] Everyone who is successful at achieving his dreams has learned that the greatest need is the need to protect his mental self.

It is estimated that the average person has between 12,000 and 70,000 thoughts a day. This is evidence enough to suggest that your goal should not be to control every thought. It is your dominant thoughts and beliefs that you must learn to bring under your conscious control as they are what largely determine your mental attitude. The Apostle Paul wrote to the church in Roman concerning the importance of guarding their thoughts:

> *And do not be conformed to this world, but be transformed by the renewing of your mind, that you may prove what is that good and acceptable and perfect will of God.* (Romans 12:2)

In essence, don't become so well-adjusted to your culture that you fit in without even thinking. Instead, fix your attention on

God. You will be changed from the inside out. You will readily recognize what He wants from you and quickly respond to it. Unlike the culture around you, always dragging you down to its level, God will bring the best out of you, developing a well-formed and informed person. You will find your random thoughts becoming more positive, purposeful, and more deliberate.

It is also important to guard your thought life because in doing so, you are protecting your internal settings. Your internal setting influences your surroundings, but it is also open to the influences of those around you. So choose your friends and those you deem as credible authorities in your life wisely. From personal experience, I can tell you that other people can influence your mental state of being to such intense levels as to throw you off into a state of disruption and/ or depression which can lead to a number of negative events.

How often are you negatively affected by someone else? Does your mood shift with your situations with them? Are your thoughts helping you; or are they giving in to the influence of another? You cannot surround yourself with people who are negative, not motivated, pessimistic and bitter and expect to be different. You must surround yourself with people who take the issues of life seriously. You must surround yourself with people who are positive, pure and actively guarding their own thought life. You must get to know them by not only what they say but also by what they do. So today, take inventory of your thoughts and the company you keep.

Our mind is an incredible gift from God. Nevertheless, it has to be managed. Maybe you can't control your circumstances at this moment, but you can control your thoughts. In the Bible, Paul wrote to the Philippians and advised them to choose to think about the good things of God:

> *Finally, brethren, whatsoever things are true, whatsoever things are honest, whatsoever things are just, whatsoever things are pure, whatsoever things are lovely, whatsoever things are of good report; if there be*

> *any virtue, and if there be any praise, think on these*
> *things.* (Philippians 4:8)

Mahatma Gandhi gives us one more critical warning to consider. He says:

> "Watch your thoughts, they become words.
> Watch your words, they become actions.
> Watch your actions, they become habits.
> Watch your habits, they become your character.
> Watch your character, it becomes your destiny."

Chapter 11

THE WAY WE WERE: THE HOMECOMING (STORY)

Kingsland, Georgia—2004

IT WAS LATE THURSDAY evening and the sun was going down. William had just arrived in town and checked into his hotel. A window in his hotel room opened onto an expansive view over the roofs and roads of the newly develop outskirts of Kingsland, Georgia, down to the double-lane highway lined with pine trees leading to his hometown of St. Marys. Busy traffic and a scene of anxious people traveling to and from work, shopping at nearby plazas and grocery stores, and famished shoppers searching for a bite to eat at the new selection of restaurants nearby. All of this was very different for William. When he left Camden County in 1984, a Naval Military Base was just commissioned two years earlier. After an impact study was completed with Congressional approval, the Secretary of the Navy announced Kings Bay, an area between Kingsland and St. Marys, as the future home of the new Trident submarine base. A few years later Kings Bay would be given a full complement of 14 to 18 fleet ballistic–missile submarines.

Such aggressive futuristic forecast would drastically change Camden County as he knew it. Prior to William leaving southeast Georgia, the small towns in the county had not yet shown any visible signs of developing or preparation for the massive changes and growth spurt that would follow such a large government initiative. It was all mind boggling to say the least.

Yet, over twenty years later, lots of changes had transpired. All the familiar landmarks were either disguised by renovations, hidden by new landmarks, or they were no longer there. The miles of wooded acreage that spanned from one city to the next were cut down to make room for the growth of an emerging economy. Nothing looked the same. Life hardly resembled the way things were when he was a boy. Everything was larger, more occupied, and unfortunately more complicated.

William remembered the smallness of the city where he grew up. Not only St. Marys, but the county and all of the cities within the county were small as well. Everyone was familiar with most families in their cities and the surrounding cities in one way or another. Back in his early years, there was only one high school in the county, no middle schools, and an elementary School in each city of the county. William would see other kids and families at either school, sports events, church, or at the Water Front in downtown St. Marys during the Christmas holidays when the local Paper Manufacturing Company would allow the city to use the railways and a decorated train and flatbed trailer to bring Santa Claus on his sled.

Santa would park his sled in front of the river at the center of the road beyond the roundabout at end of downtown. The streets would be filled with the contagious enthusiasm of anticipating kids and their parents waiting for Santa's arrival. Steps would be attached from one end of the long sleigh to the other end. Then, after a few preliminaries, Santa would begin calling all of the kids up, one by one, to give out stockings filled with sweets, small toy items, and goodies. There always seem to be enough to go around. No kid was left out. It was the highlight of each year. Everyone was acquainted with the different faces of families and kids even If they didn't know each other by name.

But now, there were thousands of new families that filled the streets and shops. William didn't recognize any of them. The mom and pop businesses and the few corner drugstores were slowly closing their doors. The Super Walmart, Winn Dixie, and Publix had come to town making them insignificant and relics of the past. Other national franchises now populated the stretches of land that were once filled with pine trees that you could see for miles. There seem to be a surge of newness electrifying the atmosphere of the county, and an undeniable revitalization that filled the air of each city. For William, it all seem to reflect his "state of mind." He couldn't sleep.

Two years had passed since reconnecting with Bishop Potter and joining his international fellowship of ministers and churches. William had been invited by Bishop Potter to share the pulpit with him at a conference held at one of the largest Baptist Churches that happened to be in his hometown's county. A coincidence— perhaps. Just another engagement—unlikely. Thrown into the waves of unpredictability, William knew he could have been asked to minister anywhere that weekend. Instead, over twenty years after being called into ministry, he found himself at the door of opportunity to speak in his hometown area for the first time. He had ministered nationwide and internationally but never in Camden County, Georgia, until then.

People in the county heard that the elder son of Bishop William Jamison Sr. was a minister, but it was just as casual as hearing the latest update on any other local who left the county after high school and moved away. Perhaps, it may have been a little more than just the "goings-on" of a friend of the family, a fellow class mate, or an ex-neighbor. Either way, no one had ever experienced his actual ministry and this would be an event that most who knew him would show up to support or to just see with their own eyes that he was indeed a minister. After all, William was on the same marquee as the well-known Presiding Bishop of the International Fellowship of Ministers and Leaders, Bishop V.M. Potter.

Early Friday morning, the opening day of the conference, William awoke preparing to take care of some errands before preparing for his message that night. He left his room, and he entered the elevator. Once inside the lobby, William exited the elevator. A man accidentally brushed up against him. He turned around to William and said, "Excuse me." William, still walking toward the front door, turned around to respond, and as he looked closer he stopped. He realized that the man who brushed against him was none other than an old classmate he had known since elementary school. His name was Roosevelt Hardaway.

William and Roosevelt greeted each other and took a seat in the dining room of the hotel. Roosevelt mentioned that he had seen the advertisement of the conference, and he was very surprised that his old friend was coming back to the area. Roosevelt said, "William, when I heard that you were one of the two conference speakers, I knew I had to see you again." William replied, "Yes, the last time we saw each other was in 1976, my last year in Camden County before I moved to Jacksonville to finish high school."

William's thoughts suddenly flashed back to their high school days. Two old friends sat in the hotel dining areas for hours reminiscing about the way they were back in their youth. They remembered playing sports together, going to after game parties, the fights they had with each other over adolescent trivialities, and the apologies that were never given because it was a sign of weakness as young men struggling with peer pressure.

William drifted for a moment while Roosevelt continued to recall different experiences they encountered. William thought about some of the terrible fights they had as friends that went unresolved. His friend stopped talking and shook William's arm. At that moment Roosevelt broke into his thoughts by saying, "Are you still here, you went awfully quiet on me?" William looked over at Roosevelt and asked, "May I make my apology to you for all the unresolved fights we had in high school?" Roosevelt answered, "Man, I forgave you and forgot about all that stuff years ago; I'm just glad to see you again my friend!"

Thinking about the way things were growing up in St. Marys, and Camden County as a whole stirred bitter-sweet emotions within William. There were some amazing experiences that helped define him as a maturing teenage. There also some regrets—some things that he wish he could undo. But he understood that all experiences are used to shape you. After an hour or so, William and his friend Roosevelt, were giggling together like they had when they were in high school. It had been a remarkable reunion. With their individual identities relaxed, the conversation was coming to a close. Two old friends recalled a time when life was simple and carefree.

The morning was passing quickly and Roosevelt needed to leave to pick up his wife who worked the night shift at the hotel. So they left the dining room and headed to the doorway of the hotel lobby. Roosevelt signaled to his wife Amanda that he was ready to go. He introduced his wife to William. She had heard all the stories about William from her husband and was pleased to finally get a chance to meet her husband's best childhood friend in person.

The feeling William got from the moment Roosevelt bumped into him, was one of being home, comfortably familiar, and connected. He hadn't felt that since they were kids. They shook hands and embraced. As Roosevelt and his wife got closer to their car, he turn around and said to William, "You know most of your classmates will be here tonight to hear you speak. They've been talking about it all week." "We're proud of you man. Who would have thought that you would follow in your father's footsteps?"

Back when William was younger, that comment would have been associated with sarcasm and seen as a belittling. But now William wore it as a badge of honor and respect. In that very moment, something in William connected the dots of his life and he realized that God had orchestrated the very prophesy He spoke to him at Major Moore's Marsh when he was a kid. The torn half Bible that turned to the page that read:

> *Before I formed you in the womb I knew you; before you were born I sanctified you; I appointed you a prophet to the nations.*

And the promise verse that was ripped out of the old worn and tattered Bible that made him feel he was personally protected by the God he heard his father preach of stated:

> *I will never leave you nor forsake you…the Lord is my helper; I will not fear. What can man do to me?*

His life was coming full circle. It was becoming clearer that the God of *how* had a detailed plan for William's life. God had been weaving the tapestry of every experience in William's life that had brought him to this point and place in time. Still there were so many unanswered questions about his other friends and classmates; so many, he couldn't gather them into any order. Even if he could, there was no-one there who could answer them. William was facing the challenge of speaking to the most personal group of his life—his classmates, those who knew him way back when. Some of whom were friends and others were not. It was as if William needed the answers to his questions as a meter to gauge how he would be received after all these years.

"Why are they really coming to the conference?" asked William. He continued thinking, "Will they see me as the minister or the teenager they once knew—remembering the way we all were back then?" That was so long ago, but he could still remember certain experiences that would be etched in his memory for life. Some experiences would be deemed embarrassing, not to mention, inappropriate for a preacher's kid with a strict religious upbringing.

William yearned for the impossible—the opportunity to speak with other classmates as he did with Roosevelt. Unfortunately, that would not be possible on this trip. He would need to leave for another speaking engagement in Tampa, Florida on Saturday. Not lingering too long on his desire to connect with old friends, he force himself to focus on the one task at hand. William needed to focus on being the man he'd evolved into—he needed to minister in the conference with the same effectiveness, and passion necessary to please God in his assignment as he always had.

The conference opened Friday night with service beginning at 7:30 p.m. It was 6:45 p.m. and William was just picked up by the transportation arranged to take him to the church. The closer they got to the church the more William's formless butterflies grew in his stomach. This was not unusual for William. This experience had become a part of his process that assured him that he was not operating in self, but rather, that he depended upon God to accomplish His purpose through him. It kept him humble. When it was time, William would summon the courage to respectfully take ownership of the experience.

As the car came to a stop in the guest parking space, William noticed that they were early, but the church was already packed, and people were still coming. He leaned forward in the back seat of the car and stared out the window. One by one his eyes caught a glimpse of familiar faces as they passed by his parked vehicle. The windows were tinted so no one could see into the car.

The senior pastor and host of the conference, Rev. Lance Robinson, opened the pastor's entrance door on the side of the church offices and sent one of his ministry assistants to escort William inside. When William enter the offices, Bishop Potter was already there. He had arrived a few minutes before William. Bishop Potter greeted William with his signature smile and a hug. After about fifteen minutes of cordial banter and going over the schedule of events for the weekend, Rev. Robinson gathered his pastoral staff to pray before they entered the sanctuary.

As they exited the pastor's office, there was a sense of unusual purpose that filled William's heart and soul. This was not just another speaking engagement, it was God's chosen moment in his life in ministry to confirm him once more in the presence of his peers. It would be a "coming into his own" of sorts. He thought to himself, "No matter what, I'm in good company, because even Jesus found it difficult to be accepted by those who knew him as the carpenter's son."

As the procession of ministers and the two guest speakers began up the walkway to the pulpit area to be seated, there was a tranquil feeling that washed over William. When they were all aligned across the platform to their assigned seats, before sitting, William looked out over the massive audience. There mixed in with the many unfamiliar faces, were classmates, friends, neighbors, and family members. There were teachers he recognized that taught him from elementary school to high school. There were church members from the denomination he grew up in who knew his family in the audience. It was a very moving moment and nothing short of breathtaking for William.

As the conference progressed to the point of the introduction of the speaker for the night, Bishop Potter stood and walked to the podium. With his stalwart persona, Bishop Potter began to speak of William and his connection with the International Fellowship of Ministers and Pastors, William's academic and ministry accomplishments, and how they met for the first time. As he looked back at William to invite him to the podium, it was as if he knew exactly what this moment meant to William. He embraced William and asked the congregation to stand and welcome him.

As William made his way to the podium, the audience erupted into heartfelt applauds and he could hear his name called out, and even his childhood nickname, "Fess" short for professor (given to him by his second oldest sister), could be faintly heard from within the audience. There was an immense sense of "Welcome home" that resounded throughout the building. The barriers between past and present withered away. If there were any doubts in William's heart about how he would be received, at that very moment they became non-existent, and he was unexpectedly filled with a new joyful awareness. He believed that he was on the brink of discovering a great truth about where the God of *how* was taking him, something that would sustain him during the years ahead.

That night William gave one of his most profound messages, and the response to the message was overwhelming. There was a joy that washed over William knowing he had championed the moment. He had participated in something divine that will alter the course of his life. Afterwards, his former teachers and classmates embraced him with tears in their eyes. One after the other they acknowledge how much the sermon touched them and how they could see the gifting of God over his life.

One of the church staff was sent to escort William to the back offices to join the other ministers for refreshments. As William was about to leave, a young man who graduated a few years behind him stopped William and asked, "How did you know this was what you were supposed to do?" William asked what did he mean and the young man said, "When did you decide that becoming a minister was for you?" William took a few moments to answer, running his fingers down the side of his face through the hairs on his chin, his light brown eyes glaring in thoughtful contemplation. Then he replied, "Probably after I spent most of my young life frustrated in my search for answers to my life situations that only God could supply. Then, I had an insatiable appetite for understanding His Word for myself. So I read every book I could get my hands on to help me interpret and understand the Bible."

The young man stood there along with the others who surrounded William after the service. It was as if they didn't want to leave for fear they may miss an important piece of the exchange. William continued, "Even then, I wasn't satisfied, so I enrolled in a Ministerial Internship Program which exposed me to every aspect of what being a minister represented." "But" William said, "If you want the short answer, I guess I wanted more people to know what I discovered to be true about God, and about how He really does have a master plan for our lives. Besides, every answer I ever needed I found in this book—holding up his Bible. It just seemed right, natural, and only thing I was meant to do. Nothing else ever gave me as much satisfaction."

William turned to leave with his escort, waving goodbye to all who came to meet and greet him after the service. The new layers of William unraveled before them that night. It left William wondering, "What were their final impression of him?" In the weeks that would follow, he would receive letters and emails expressing their sentiments. To his public school teachers, they were delighted and filled with pride because he was one of their students that found his place in life and making a profound contribution to society. His classmates saw the friend, the neighbor, or the acquaintance of their youth who beat the odds and transcended the limitations of a small town with grace and humility. There was no doubt in their mind that he was where he should be, and that ministry was his destiny.

Chapter 12

CONFRONTING THE PROS AND CONS OF FAMILIARITY

*The aspects of things that are most important for us are hidden
because of their simplicity and familiarity.*
~ Ludwig Wittgenstein

Familiarity and Relationships

IF WE ARE HONEST with ourselves, we all have the need to connect
with others, especially those who are like us in some way. What
draws us to others is intriguing, and it varies from person to person.
Like myself, there are some, who have the type of personality that
give them the knack of winning people over with their positive
attitude and understanding nature.

We encounter many people every day; however, we allow very
few to get close in a relationship. Some last a lifetime while others
choose to withdraw for reasons best known to them, leaving behind
their imprint long after they have gone. The common questions that
I encounter at my seminars on *Life, Love, and Relationships* are,
"What nurtures and/or damages a friendship or a relationship?" I

offer several possibilities. But regardless of my answer, I always confront them with the reality that when a relationship ends we are left wondering if we have given too much of ourselves in the process. In other words, did we become too familiar?

At one point or another, we will all find ourselves on an emotional roller coaster. One moment we are experiencing happiness and joy, and the next, pain or fear. Our minds have

> Never compromise who you really are just to be validated by others.

the unique capability of excavating memories and creating visuals like a film loop running in our heads that replays everything that ever went wrong in the past while conveniently omitting all the good and positive experiences, such as, arguments we had with our close relative or the guilt from careless comments we made to a close friend. The experiences leave us lying awake at night, *what-If-ing* ourselves into a seemingly unredeemable restlessness. We construct calamitous and unlikely possibilities, and then treat them as if they were real. Those negative messages clutter our self-confidence; undermine our will to go on; and if we are not careful, we can get lost in the person we're expected to be for the sake of acceptance. That's one of the major down-sides of familiarity.

Love and respect close friends with all your heart but never compromise who you really are just to be validated by others. Be authentic, especially with the person you're intimate with. It is difficult to be intimate with another while hiding or denying your true feelings and desires from them. Know your personal value system, and live by it while understanding that a certain degree of transparency should exist in all close relationships. Transparency is the ability to be completely open and vulnerable to another without the fear of maltreatment or rejection. When you stop sharing, the whole essence of the friendship is lost.

So, once you get to know yourself—who you really are, and find that peace within, automatically people will be drawn to you and wish to be friends. In this atmosphere of openness and trust, it will be a relief to have at least one true person in this society that won't use the transparency against you. There is no avoiding it, and there is no substitute for it. Transparency is necessary to deem yourself worthy of being called a close friend

Familiarity and Personal Success

In Chapter 11, William was faced with the unknown effects and expectations of familiarity. After leaving the rural area of southeast Georgia as a teenager, he was invited back as a guest speaker in a county-wide conference. This would be the first time he would come face-to-face as an adult and as a minister with childhood friends, classmates, and teachers.

The concern William had was, could they receive him as an evolved adult and minister? Would he still walk in the shadow of the teenager last remembered in the late seventies? He was the preacher's kid, the young boy rejected as a nerd turned teenage athlete—popular and eventually accepted by all. The guy who, for a moment, became a *bad boy* rebelling against his father in high school who eventually ran away from home—the basketball player who unexpectedly left school at the end of his eleventh grade school year to move to Jacksonville to finish twelfth grade.

His concerns about familiarity were valid, but not worthy of giving in to them and exposing himself to their potential distraction. Fortunately, William's experience in his hometown was exceptional and was a pivotal moment in his life and ministry.

Familiarity is a common distraction to success. For many individuals, it is difficult to get beyond the mindset of, "As I knew him." Ironically, that phrase appears after the death of a person during his funeral as a program item under the guise of tributes. In many respects, I think it is a wonderful act of kindness on behalf of close friends and family. On the other hand, there are many who may be in the very same setting that have quite the opposite perception of the person whose life they are celebrating. These perceptions are usually based on a different level of familiarities and biases. The advantage of familiarity is reality–both good and bad. The disadvantage is, we disburse our positive energy onto those we know least (a visiting speaker, a new neighbor, a new acquaintance, etc.) and we express our negative or less complementary energy with those we know best.

Before you totally disagree, allow me to submit for your consideration a few definitions and a personal supposition. I chose to use the definition of familiarity from three different sources to bring clarity to the direction of this chapter:

a. The better we know people, the more likely we are to find fault with them. - *The New Dictionary of Cultural Literacy*
b. If you know someone very well or experience something a lot, you stop respecting them. - *The Free Dictionary*
c. The more you know something or someone, the more you start to find faults and dislike things about it or them. - *UsingEnglish.com*

As a minister, when I speak publically, my words are filtered through my knowledge of God's Word, and my experiences which established the Kingdom principles in my life I have come to know as truth. Because of that, I believe what I have to say matters. Yet, that is relative. There are those who are familiar with me as a childhood friend or acquaintance. They were privy to my personal quirks, and flaws. According the definition of familiarity, they could be less likely to embrace me seriously as a minister as others do. On the other hand, individuals who know less of my earlier life would more likely view me as an evolved man, father and minister, and would be more likely to hold me as a credible authority and more apt to readily receive me as a minister more seriously. The same is possible of those who have unrealistic expectations of those who do or don't fit into certain categories in life.

Socio-economic status, nationality, level of education, personality differences and experiences, the failure and success rate of a person, the number of good versus bad decisions made, and questionable experiences all represent some of the many variables that influence how people perceive you. Your level of interaction with them determines their level of familiarity with you.

> **Familiarity is a common ignored distraction to success.**

We live in a familiar world with familiar dangers within boundaries. The dangers are when familiarity creates permanent biases, when one's inability to change is dismissed, or when it impedes the growth, promotion, and performance of others. The key to a door that needs to be opened in someone's life could be within reach, however, if the person who holds the key is disqualified because of one familiarity issue or another, his blessings or his being a blessing to someone can be forfeited. This is not a new dilemma.

Case and Point:

(Mark 6:3 KJV) *Is not this the carpenter, the son of Mary, the brother of James, and Joses, and of Juda, and Simon? And are not his sisters here with us?* ***And they were offended at him***. In Israel, carpentry was an insignificant occupation. While working in metals was considered an art, carpentry was a part-time trade. The carpenter used a few crude tools, fixed broken doors or plows, made wooden spoons and wooden door keys, and shaped rude tables and chairs. In the East, houses were constructed of stone or mud bricks, and most household dishes were of pottery. There was little need for the skilled work done by modern carpenters. Thus, to call Jesus a carpenter was to dismiss Him as one who followed an insignificant trade, as today one might say, he is just a "day laborer."

How could Jesus be the Messiah they thought? Who gave Him the right to teach us anything from the Torah? What is this other teaching? It is not in the books of the Law? How dare He teach anything other than what God has given us? How could He be the Son of God? He's a heretic! They knew too much about Him and His family. They scoffed at Him saying, "Can anything good come out of Nazareth?" These are all questions that signal the dangers of familiarity.

Where a person comes from, his history, his career choices, etc. does not disqualify him from being used by God, nor does it disqualify him from being of benefit to society in whatever career path he chooses to serve in. People can change. Every one of us was born with the potential to evolve into a better person— to become who we were predestined to be. Unfortunately, the average human being learns to rate and compartmentalize people and relationships at an early age. Distinctions are developed, ripening into a distinction, between familiar and unfamiliar. Boundaries are then established creating the confusion between familiarity and the ability to trust. One does not necessary equate to the other.

Avoid the Confusion

Familiarity is an unavoidable fact of life, and trust is a solution for specific problems of risk. But, trust has to be achieved within a familiar world, in a familiar community, and in familiar relationships. As changes occur, and they will, the familiar features of the world in which we live and the people we interact with will have an impact on the possibility of developing trust in our human relations with them. Hence, we cannot neglect the conditions and dangers of familiarity and its limits when we set out to explore the conditions of trust.[1] After all, it was these very conditions that led to the Jewish nation missing the coming of their Messiah, forfeiting their blessing, and their eyes being blinded to the truth. As John the Apostle expressed, *He came to His own, and His own did not receive Him* (John 1:11 NKJV).

They didn't respect Him because they knew His family. They could not accept Jesus because of where He grew up. They could not move beyond Jesus' previous insignificant profession as a common laborer, *Isn't this the carpenter?* (Mark 6:3 KJV). They probably thought to themselves, "Jesus? Our Messiah? King of the Jews? Yeah, right?!" If they did it to the Son of God, it is conceivable that those who think they know you could miss the amazing person you are in God. You may not be there yet. Perhaps you are still in the process—still in the Potter's hand. He is shaping you every day to become who you are to be. So don't allow other people's opinions of you to stunt your growth. Declare who you are in God's eyes every day, and keep moving forward.

Familiarity Can Breed Contempt

We develop methods to interpret or size people up by actions or characteristics, such as, the hidden side of individuals, the nature of how others process or respond to life situations, the unexpected surprises that are revealed the closer you become, the inaccessibility of another's thoughts unless they are expressed, and the complexity of their personality affect our perception and acceptability of them. In essence, the more information people have about others, the more likely their opinions will change about them which in turns determine whether or not they like and/or accept them.

This selection process creates a positive correlation between knowledge and liking across the set of one's acquaintances, but it may also lead individuals to believe that more knowledge causes greater liking within any given acquaintanceship. It is suggested that the relationship between knowledge and liking within individuals is in fact negative: that more information about any one person leads, on average, to less liking for that person. It is further suggested that this relationship is due to the lure of ambiguity or uncertainty. At first acquaintance, individuals read into others what they wish and find evidence of similarity, leading to liking.[2]

> Declare who you are in God's eyes every day and keep moving forward.

Unfortunately, the driving connection between familiarity and dislike is a lack of similarity. We are instinctively drawn to people who are like us. Once we become familiar with people and perceive dissimilarity, it's all downhill from there. Even traits we might have liked, or been neutral about before, now get the thumbs down. We have all experienced this at one point or another in our life. It begins as a child growing up with other siblings, especially in a large family. Each sister and brother, having the same parents, exemplifies very different personalities. Although they may share the same home environment, the same last name, the same parents, and attend the same church, the older they get in that same environment, the more they will discover their differences. As they grow up together, they will begin to notice those with similar likes and dislikes form attachments and spend more time together than with the others.

When trouble arises among the siblings, the support and defense groups among them become more apparent based on their connection. Likewise, you see the same reaction in friendships, associates on your job, relationships at church, and affiliates in business. It is a normal human characteristic. It is in our universal DNA to be drawn to others like us. We do actually meet people who turn out to be similar to us who end up as our close friends or even partners. But even with such relationships, the closer they become, the more they will discover their differences and underlying quirks.

It is at that point, our personal constitution is put to the test. I counsel couples, families, and individuals all the time who get lost in the confusion of familiarity, trust, and betrayal. I assist them in understanding that while familiarity is necessary to build any relationship, it is also the doubled edged sword. The Bible admonishes us to:

> *Know those who labor among you, and are over you in the Lord...* (1 Thessalonians 5:12)

But it also makes us aware that, *A man's foes shall be they of his own household* (Matthew 10:36). This is because they have all the goods on you! They know things about you that outsider don't know. They know your strengths and your weaknesses. They know what you like and what you don't like. They know exactly what mental and emotional buttons to push and make you vulnerable. Outsiders don't have such an advantage unless they are being advised by someone who is that close to you.

You are supposed to be able to trust those closest to you. Yes, familiarity is still at the base level, a must in building relationships. The advantages and disadvantages are what we all must contend with. Hopefully, the more we understand it the better we are able to find the delicate balance needed to maintain and nurture relationships properly.

Where there is an inability to manage the information we are privy to in an ever evolving relationship, there will be a need to experience the person we first met or fell in love with (a close friend, a boyfriend, or a life partner, etc.). It is the basic need to experience the familiar. As the relationships reveal the different layers of the person, there is always a point where you are introduced to an undesirable trait/s that tends to disappoint. We either embrace the more desirable traits, make known to the person how the less desirable ones affect us (if it is an issue and worth addressing), or we get stuck on the less desirable trait/s and begin to define the person by it.

Thus the theory is that people would rather not know, than to know and be disappointed. The vast majority of the people I have interviewed over the past ten years of counseling confessed that the less they know about someone the more they are inclined to like them. The rationale behind this has more to do with the old idiom. "What you don't know won't hurt you." On the surface I thought I understood this saying. It seemed simple enough. If you have no knowledge about whatever it is that would be a potential disagreeable quality, threat, or problem for you, then you have no reason to worry about it.

But, the idiom has a deeper meaning than the implied advantage of just not knowing. When you apply the idiom to relationships what you get is a different bent on the conclusion. There is a certain perceived advantage tied to this level of ambiguity. This level of relational ambiguity allows us to imagine that other people share our world-view, our personality traits, or our sense of humor. Unfortunately, as soon as, we start to find out more about them, we're likely to find out how different they are to ourselves and, as a result, to dislike them and/or treat them differently.

Familiarity Can Breed Complacency

Familiarity can also be comfortable. It makes us feel secure and content which leads to blind faith. Trust leads to greater satisfaction and commitment to a relationship, but it can also lead to complacency and acceptance of less-than-satisfactory outcomes from such a relationship.[3]

As a minister and counselor, I have spent over thirty years working with countless number of families. Having the opportunity to work three and a half years in the inner city of Rivera Beach, Florida while working on my doctorate degree in counseling, I experienced a substantial number of crisis cases. I tend to think that nothing much would be able to surprise me anymore. But perhaps, it is in familiarity that danger lurks. Because of familiarity, like most counselors, at times, we tend to blind ourselves from the distinctions that could actually be critical to our clients' welfare and safety. We fool ourselves with past templates that could fit our clients' experience, making them more similar than unique. Families and people are very similar, but they are also unique.

My experiences working in the inner-city revealed an important principle about familiarity's complacency. The streets were always patrolled. There was a constant increase in neighborhood watch groups, and the residents' lives were becoming less private and more endangered. They were on edge, and they were concerned as their neighborhoods begin to change into a constant war-zone. They worried at every turn that some evil might lurk in a hidden corner where they least expected it. They planned their activities with greater detail and varied their daily regimen a bit to be a little less predictable. After years of dealing with the conditions, it became a way of life for them, and complacency set in—and although unpleasant, familiarity made them content.

They were facing real enemies that threatened their way of life: drugs, gang violence, prostitution, rapes, murders, etc. But, the longer I worked and studied the environment; I had to ask the questions: Who was the true enemy? Why did the security patrols diminish? What caused the neighborhood watch groups to cease? After talking with long-term residents who knew the area before a publicized assessment deemed it an "at-risk" community, I realized that the many destructive factions named above could justifiably be labeled as the enemy. However, of all the multifaceted dangers that presented themselves; complacency became their biggest adversary.

> When we settle for less, we eventually begin to feel confident the situation is stable. We forget that things can get worse.

It was a city that fell prey to external influences, eventually destroying the local residents' way of life. But, this condition is as lethal to individuals as it was to that city. I returned to Riviera Beach years later. I found the city of West Palm Beach had begun what was called a "Beautification Program." They were slowly buying up property that fell victim to drugs and all of the residual effects that usually follow. Block by block, they demolished building after building and extended the police patrols further into the once devalued areas. As I rode through the different sub-divisions, it was if I had entered a new world. Nothing looked the same. Renovations were taking place. New buildings were erected, and the roads were being widened. All that was needed was a fresh new outlook, a plan, and executing the necessary changes to make it happen.

Familiarity can breed a self-satisfied state of mind that will make you oblivious to anything lurking in the crevices of your life that could hinder your forward movement. We regularly experience complacency in our personal lives and at our jobs. The key is being conscious of its existence and the actions we can take to offset any negative consequences.

The places we find ourselves feeling most familiar with in life, whether they are relational, financial, educational, or emotional, can be the most perilous because the menace is not so obvious to us. When we settle for less, we eventually begin to feel confident the situation is stable. We often forget things are subject to change for the worse and progressively become perilous. We must learn to respond and interact with our surroundings to ensure that we are alert to the possibilities of diminishing success, loss of interest in your future dreams, or failing relationships.

Familiarity's complacency is an attitude that determines how we respond to any given situation. I remember pastoring my first church. I was a church planter in my earlier years of ministry, but this particular church was not one that I'd planted, however it was well established. I had been assigned there because the previous pastor was removed for reasons that were not disclosed to me. After serving as pastor a few months, it became clear that changes needed to be made. The church was in survival mode prior to my assignment. They were losing members and the finances were reflecting the lost.

I remember establishing an advisory committee to begin looking at a proposal I submitted to resolve the issues confronting the declining state of the church. A church conference was convened to take a vote on implementing the proposed changes. What I experienced during the church conference that night was the same grid-lock banter and dialogue I'd heard when I was a child during my father's church meetings when he wanted to implement something new. How many times have you heard the statement, "We have always done it that way?" Needless to say, that is exactly what I got as they voted against the critical changes that I proposed that needed to be made.

I eventually transitioned out of that church, and I moved on to a new assignment. I have learned that you can't make people change. As I stated earlier, familiarity is comfortable. Some may say, "Of course, it must be right if it has stood the test of time and repetitiveness." But, I strongly suggest that, this kind of thinking is not necessarily true! The very fact it is repeated often can draw us into the complacency trap. We learn to expect what we have always experienced (good, bad, or indifferent) until one day, the outcome changes for the worse.

We must learn that change is critical for any progress to take place. Our relationships with each other, our business relationships, and our relationship with God, they are all subject to change. We can miss divine moments in our lives because we become so familiar with God and His word that we take Him for granted. It is the same way we may take a friend, a sibling, a parent, or spouse for granted. When that happens, we allow the poisonous emotions, feelings, and behaviors to seed into the soil of our mind and develop within us.

As it was with Jesus, after preaching the messages concerning the Kingdom of God, the healings, the feeding, the raising of the dead, and all the other miracles that could not be recorded, they celebrated Him as He rode through town on His way to Jerusalem on the back of a donkey. They cried, *Hosanna, hosanna: Blessed is the King of Israel that cometh in the name of the Lord.* But once He was betrayed and accused of a crime against Rome, they shouted, *Crucify Him, crucify Him!*

The danger of familiarity will cause people to celebrate you when you are on the same page with them, but when the tides of life change, with the same breath that celebrated you, they will curse you.

Why? They do it out of ignorance, jealousy, and some even think they really are doing it for some inherent good. We can learn from Jesus' response on Golgotha, after He experienced the pain of betrayal, the physical and emotional torture, and finally the burden and humiliation of the cross when He said, *Father, forgive them; for they know not what they do* (Luke 23:34 KJV). It is at the cross where we must all submit the double-edge sword of familiarity and all who fall prey to it. Only then can we experience the freedom to succeed and fulfill our destiny in life.

Part III

Understanding Life's Triumphs

Chapter 13

ONCE MORE TO LIVE (STORY)

When defeat comes, accept it as a signal that your plans are not sound,
rebuild those plans, and set sail once more toward your coveted goal.
~ Napolean Hill

Boca Raton, Florida 2006

BACK TO EARTH. HE fell, with a thud, back into the reality of this "new" chapter of life he classified as "the norm" after his world came crashing down several years earlier. This was his first speaking engagement in the islands since 1991. A ferry from St. John, Virgin Islands to St. Thomas; from there, a commuter plane to San Juan, Puerto Rico with a connecting flight to Miami, and finally the drive back to Boca Raton. Flying was not his favorite means of transportation, so William put on his head phones and mentally zoned out during his commute to help ease the normal thoughts he would have of crashing. William imagined flying north, like migrating birds returning to their natural habitat, but for William, he was returning home to Boca Raton.

As he pulled into the parking garage of his condominium, he was met by the reality of his weekly routine of counseling sessions, at-risk community meetings, mid-week bible class preparations, and finalizing projects to plan; the thought of his responsibilities all reaching out to him and clinging like pieces of light debris on a static filled sweater pulled from a hot dryer. Ministry in the inner city and working with the regeneration centers were quite demanding. William had become somewhat of an ambassador of hope for the distressed families where he served in Riviera Beach. Routine court appearance with one member or another, weekly hospital visit to pray with afflicted members, and visits to the rehabilitation center to bring words of encouragement to an addicted patient at the request of a family member who attended his church were the norm for William, but it was a labor of love. After years of redefining where he and his ministry fit, it made him feel like his life mattered.

He awoke early the next morning, just before sunrise, after returning from his week-long speaking engagement in the Virgin Islands. It was still dark outside, and everything felt a little topsy-turvy. Throughout the night, a long-held list of things-to-do clung to his mind, so William decided to immerse himself into his work. As the sun began to peak through the darkness, William did his best to ignore the temptation to abandon work and take a ride to Mizner Park in east Boca Raton near the beach to get a cup of espresso and hangout for a bit. The beach there was an amazing scene of serenity early in the morning before the beach goers arrived and would be worth the distraction and delay of work.

But, William passed on the temptation and continued working through his list of scheduled tasks. By mid-day, most of the paperwork portion of his tasks was completed. He rose from the desk in his home office to take a break. He walked over to the sliding glass door that looked onto his veranda and pressed his forehead on the cool glass door as he used to do when he was a young boy—when he couldn't go outside to play because his chores were not finished.

During his break time, William watched his neighbors for a while; like clockwork the same group of five would walk the same route each day before they prepared to leave for their offices. They seem to admire the same yards and stop at the same points of interest each day. Perhaps it was an intentional measure of distance that determined the stops. Behind the group, as if it were a standing appointment, a young couple followed, wheeling their new baby down the street. They halted every few steps to talk or make adjustments. Everyone in the group circled the carriage, leaning into the baby's face, making noises, and praising the baby. The proud parents seemed to really enjoy the attention.

William enjoyed the entertainment of watching them each day. Perhaps, transitioning from his former life, they represented some sense of stability and normalcy. Like other people whose lives had been irretrievably altered by some unfortunate experience or event, William wanted to comfort himself by assuming that his life could resume its former course, but the reality was clear, there was no way his life would return to its old track. William would soon discover that God is always up to something new.

The mail carrier passed the group of neighbors and headed to the community mailboxes. William made his way into the kitchen to put on a kettle of hot water for his tea. He decided to go check his mail while waiting for the water to heat up. His neighbors had retrieved their mail and were making their way back home. William pulled out his mail, and as he sorted through the junk mail and bills, he noticed that he had received a letter from Dr. Travis Colson, chancellor of Xavier Christian University.

This seemed peculiar because all of his previous communications with the chancellor had been minimal (a greeting and brief banter) when William would visit the university for meetings on behalf of the alumni association. William was voted in as President of the Alumni Association one year after he completed his graduate studies. The assignment kept him in touch with the university and former students, and he attended periodic meetings annually. During those trips, he was privy to see Dr. Colson from time to time, but to receive a personal letter from the chancellor was totally unexpected.

As William began walking back to his home, he opened the letter and began to read its content. He realized that this was an invitation for him to consider serving as Vice President at Large for the university. William froze in his steps…speechless. It took him back for a minute or two. It never occurred to him that he was standing in the middle of the road and had not made it back to the house until the radio of a passing car got his attention. "Wow!" He thought to himself, "Is this real? Is this really happening?" The content of the letter was unconceivable and refreshing all at the same time. It was like getting up at dawn and seeing the sun rise while the rest of the world still slept.

William finally made it back inside. He slowly prepared the tea and headed back to his home office as the tea was steeping. He gently laid the letter down on his desk as if it were pages from a fragile antiquity of ancient writings taken from the lost books of the Bible. He sat back in his desk chair in pure disbelief. It had been a struggle for William to reestablish himself after watching two decades of his life and ministry collapse around him. Although he had experienced small recovery moments, like his connection with Bishop V.M. Potter and the homecoming conference in St. Marys, he still wrestled with himself to hold on to the small pieces of inspiration that kept him waking up each day. He was cautiously optimistic as he followed the new path that was unfolding year by year despite all the voices telling him that his "comeback" was impossible, and that he would never have the future he relinquished when he left the religious denomination where he was once licensed as a minister.

Prior to receiving the letter, he had learned to pretend that perhaps such heights were meant for other people who didn't have his past, or his flaws—people who deserved it because they made all the right decisions with minimal failures. Each night William would pray to be spared from a fate that would place a lid over his future. He felt there was so much more his life was meant for. Yet these pretend thoughts lit up his mind in the darkness of each passing night. It was as if he entertained these pretend thoughts to buffer himself from any disappointments the future held for him. At least he would have an excuse for not achieving the things he so boldly professed when he was younger. Perhaps that's not quite true, but those were his thoughts, and he kept them secret. No one knew of his private inner struggles.

Every now and then, when he was feeling hopelessly stalled, William would Google his own name. No matter how often he did this, it surprised him that he was still alive and well on the internet. While this practice may not have been common place, perhaps it was—he didn't know, and he didn't care; all he knew was that it was refreshing to know that a lapse in his life and his ministry did not erase him from the world entirely. God was watching over William and in His own timing, He would continue to reveal more new chapters in William's life.

Four years earlier, William finished his doctorate degree, fulfilling a long term educational goal. He restored his relationship with his father—a surprising turn of events, he connected with the International Fellowship of Pastors and Ministers, and received his Ordained Minister certification and licensure. Now, William was invited to become an executive of the university where he attended graduate school and was President of the Alumni Association. His dreams, though on a different path, were becoming a reality. In fact, where God was taking William exceeded his own dreams.

One week later, after receiving the letter from Chancellor Colson, his executive assistant phoned William to say that the chancellor wanted to meet with him to discuss the details of the position. An appointment was set for the meeting to convene after the chancellor returned for his trip to Argentina. For William, this was a major opportunity. Dr. Travis Colson was known worldwide not only as the founder and chancellor of Xavier Christian University, but also as founder and president of Xavier Global Network, which was a network of churches, para-churches, educational and humanitarian organizations working in twenty-six nations. William had been offered an opportunity to be in this influential arena—working side-by-side with this iconic visionary.

William's life was about to be punctuated with another piece of the divine puzzle that was strategically coming together. He was on the brink of turning another unexpected corner, changing his life completely as if someone waved a magic wand and completely altered his destiny. He had an intense sense of how far he had come since that introspective night in a hotel room in Atlanta, Georgia when he came face-to face with some tough personal truths about himself. Life had been confusing, challenging, and difficult. William was confident things would get better and that he would have another chance at experiencing life differently. He was hoping with every passing day that heaven was pulling the pendulum back a little bit further, and upon God's timely nod it would strongly swing in the other direction—God's true north, His divine favor. Several years later, it had done just that. Though he will always remain in the balance of the inevitable fortune and misfortune of destiny's ever-unfolding characteristic, right now, for William, life felt especially sweet.

Jacksonville, Florida

The day had come for William to meet with Dr. Colson at the Xavier Christian University in the Regency area of Jacksonville. He arrived in town early Friday morning and drove straight to the executive offices. William parked his car and proceeded to walk into the building. As he was striding down the corridor, he was met by the receptionist. It appeared she was on her way back from the break room area. She greeted William with a "Good morning" as she placed her morning cup of coffee and pastry on her desk.

"Good morning to you." William replied. The receptionist asked William's name and how could she help him. William responded, "I'm Dr. William Jamison II, and I have a meeting scheduled with the Dr. Colson at 9:30, but I am a little early." The receptionist asked

William to have a seat and made known his presence to the executive assistant to the chancellor. A few minutes later, he was led back to Dr. Colson's office. William's heart drummed with anticipation and a little nervousness the closer they got to the chancellor's office.

Oblivious to William's trepidation, the executive assistance seemed thrilled as though the chancellor had informed her of the purpose of his visit. Once in his office, the assistant seated William and offered him coffee or tea to drink. He said, "No thank you, I'm fine." His heightened anticipation would not allow him to eat or drink before the meeting. The assistant replied, "Okay, the chancellor will be with you in a moment. He's concluding another meeting."

After waiting for about five minutes, William calmed his racing thoughts and steadied himself for the meeting with the chancellor. He sat there wondering what to say and how to greet the chancellor— would there be an entourage of people that would follow him from the meeting? But when Dr. Colson entered his office, William saw no executive envoy, no assistant anxiously trotting in behind him with files or paperwork under one arm needing his signature and the other arm extended with a hot cup in her hand—anticipating his need for hot coffee without asking. That is not what William saw. He saw a humbled man with gray hair and a soothing light-toned voice, who gently asked him to please have a seat when William sprang from his chair to greet him.

Dr. Colson came over to William and shook his hand and asked if his trip was uneventful and safe. William replied that the trip was uneventful and that he was thrilled to be there. After all the pleasantries were exchanged between the two of them, Dr. Colson paused for a moment as if he was politely waiting on William to finish a thought. William leaned forward as though continuing the conversation and said, "What a splendid honor sir, to be considered for such a position." Dr. Colson, with a confused look on his face asked, "What position?" William was slow to respond but thought to himself, "Did he misunderstand the invitation? Was the position filled and he not contacted?" His mind began racing a million miles a second, but Dr. Colson put William's mind quickly at ease. "Just kidding," he said.

His face glowing as pink as sunrise and his hands fluttering like doves, Dr. Colson reiterated that he was just kidding. I guess he saw the shock and awe in William's face. William slid back and lowered himself in his chair and laughed in relief. It was refreshing to witness a man of the chancellor's stature who had remained so down to earth and with an invigorating sense of humor. "Tell me Dr. Jamison, have you had enough time to consider my invitation to be Vice President at Large?" Dr. Colson asked. William replied, "Yes, I have. It is all I could think about over the past two weeks." He sighed and continued, "Actually, it is quite overwhelming."

"Well Dr. Jamison," Dr. Colson said, "I've been inquiring about you and keeping abreast of your ministry since you graduated with us a few years ago. You impressed us as a student and your graduate school mentor Dr. Thomas Roberts advised me that you were someone to keep close to the university. This is why your name was submitted, and you were voted in as President of the Alumni Association. We have been pleased with your contribution to the university over the past few years."

Dr. Colson continued, "More recently, I had the opportunity to speak with an associate of mine who is familiar with the work that you're doing in the Palm Beach County area. What you've accomplished in the inner-city of Riviera as a pastor is exceptional. The book you published, *By the Way*, which was a testament to your commitment to the mission of the Gospel, the necessity of education, and the importance of change was compelling. You are the kind of person we need to assume the Vice President at Large position at the university." Dr. Colson continued, "We want you to do on a larger scale what you have done in the inner city. Your role will be to champion the cause of Christian Education on a regional level, to identify and plant potential extension campuses, and to represent the university on my behalf when I am unable to."

William's light brown eyes were fixed on Dr. Colson as he sat across the desk from him, item after item, laying out the involved role and responsibilities of the position being offered to him. William was moved by the extent of confidence and trust being bestowed upon him by the chancellor and the university. Dr. Colson asked William again if he was sure that this would be something he would be interested in. William replied, "Yes! Yes, it will be an honor to serve the university in this capacity." He never dreamt that his calling in life would place him on this particular path, never presumed. Yet God, whom he enthusiastically now refers to as the God of *how*, chose to grace a small town boy, flawed, and still finding his way back in life with such an honor.

The meeting ended in a prayer of consecration of sorts and with Chancellor Colson laying his hands upon William's head and speaking a blessing over his new assignment. William was introduced to the staff and volunteers as the new Vice President at Large. Everyone seemed very pleased to have him on board.

With no stops other than to gas up and pick up a sandwich to go, William traveled back to Boca Raton that same day. During the drive home, he replayed the events of the day in his head. By late evening he was settled in at home, still in awe of what had transpired earlier in the day. That night, William huddled in the arms of his favorite recliner looking through the skylight of his veranda. He peered into the star-lit skies, thanking God for what was unfolding in his life at that moment.

Although William was pastoring, he had been training different lay ministers to assume some of the day-to-day responsibilities of the ministry. His recent assignment with the university would require more of his time, and William would eventually have to assign one of his associates as the new pastor of the church. This would be as much of a shock to those who have come to know William as it was to William himself. But as time passed, they all only wanted what was best for William. He continued to teach weekly for about two months before transitioning the new leadership into their roles. It was a bitter-sweet moment for everyone, but they knew that this day would come.

Several months later, William officially assumed the post of Vice President at Large for Xavier Christian University. It was still difficult for him to fathom the chain of events that led up to this moment. It was a mystery to him. He never sought such stations in life or dreamed of walking the lofty path of academia, yet they came. All he ever wanted was to know the ways of wisdom and grace, and walk them the best he could. He had always believe that if he followed the path of what was right and what was noble, whatever God had for his life would come to pass.

In the first week at the university, William felt like he had stepped into one of those amazing dreams that you never want to awake from. Initially, he sensed his presence would be treated like a curiosity—"What kind of university leader would he become?" or "Will he be able to transition from being a pastor to an executive educator?" But it wasn't long before he went from being their new associate to being their Vice President at Large. As time passed, he found his place and his true voice in the arena of academia.

As he settled into his position, William quickly realized that nothing could have prepared him for the life that was unfolding before him—not for the intensity of joy he would experience, nor for the depth of fulfillment that would also come through his work with the university. He fell in love with his newfound career of educating future ministers, laymen, pastors, and establishing affiliate campuses. He was visiting churches around the southeast region of the nation. His speaking engagements increased to record heights, and he was in demand to give presentations at seminars and conferences.

It seems William had come a long way toward answering the questions we all need answered no matter what pains we suffered. He believed one day his story would help others make the journey from tragedy and grief back to life. He understood his story was not original, but along his journey he began to share with others that sometimes when we're suffering we feel as if we're singled out. We often wonder why God has picked on us. But his life over the past ten years taught him that if that's what we think, we are mistaken. He came to realize that he was never alone in his suffering, and that God's choice of allowing experiences of suffering were not arbitrary, but purposeful. In the end, if you allow Him, God will work everything according to His master plan for your life, and it will be for your good, and it will be beautiful. It will be your dream come true.

We grow great by dreams. All big men are dreamers.
They see things in the soft haze of a spring day,
Or in the red fire of a long winter's evening.

Some of us let these great dreams die, but others
Nourish and protect them, nurse them through bad days
Till they bring them to the sunshine and light...
Which come always to those who sincerely hope
That their dreams will come true.
~ Woodrow Wilson

Chapter 14

BEHIND THE CURTAIN OF CAUSE (A TAPESTRY OF EXPERIENCES)

JOURNALIZING WILLIAM JAMISON II's life experiences was much like walking with a ghost. It was a journey through a mysterious wilderness with no guide to direct the next steps of the sightseer. There were so many experiences that contributed to the shaping of his life, choosing only a few was most difficult. However, behind each story lie the mystery that bares the question of what fueled the cause for each dilemma or situation. Cause, to understand it, one must implore its companion "effect." Cause and effect notes the relationship between actions and events such that one or more are the result of the other or others. Simply stated, a cause is "Why" something happens, and the effect is "What" happens. Behind the curtain of cause lies the enigmatic motive of creation, purpose— God's overall intention or His predetermined, inevitable, irresistible, course of events to fulfill a divine plan.

In His master plan for creation, there are volumes of books that chronicles His plans. Every individual born in this world has his own book in the volume of books. This personalized book of yours has a unique and detailed plan for your reason to be born. Jesus revealed this part of creation's mystery when, in a conversation with God—His Father, He said:

> *Therefore when he came into the world, He said, Sacrifice and offering You did not desire, but a body You have prepared for Me: In burnt offerings and sacrifices for sin You had no pleasure. Then I said, Behold, I have come—in the **volume of the book** it is written of Me, to do Your will, O God.* (Hebrews 10:5-7 NKJV)

If that wasn't enough insight to inspire you or at the very least, to make you feel some level of personal value to God, here is another slice of truth. God Himself says, *the counsel of the Lord stands forever, the plans of His heart to all generations* (Psalms 33:11 NKJV). Every generation of people that have ever lived and that will ever be born, come into this world with a book written in heaven. Hence, every experience in the world have a predetermined outcome also recorded. Because every human has been given the gift of "free will," we have the proclivity toward choosing to operate either inside or outside the *will* of God; which mean, you will either live in God's perfect will or if you choose to—you can exist in His permitted will.

A cause is *why* something happens. An effect is *what* happens.

This is a very involved theological concept, but I have given you enough to understand that absolutely nothing in life is an arbitrary crap shoot. There is a God, and He has an intentional progressive plan for all of His creation. Every experience allowed in our lives have a general divine purpose of keeping or getting us back on track with God's intention for us. There is a deeper more profound purpose, but that is between you and God. In His own timing, He will reveal it to you.

Marcus Aurelius Antonius Augustus, Emperor of the Roman Empire from 161 to his death in 180, said, "What we do now echoes in eternity." I'm not sure if the Emperor understood the depth and far reaching implications of his statement, but it was validated by John, the Revelator. He wrote:

> *And I saw the dead, small and great, standing before God; and the books were opened: and another book was opened, which is **the Book** of Life: and the dead were judged according to their works, by the things which were written in the books.* (Revelation 20:12 NKJV)

The sum total of your experiences and what you accomplish or not, will be weighed and balanced by what God has written in His book concerning you and your purpose.

It bares to reason that if we don't know and understand these theological trues, the experiences we go through will at times seem so wasteful and unnecessary. We are left with this tiresome feeling that questions the *why* of life. When there is a lack of understanding *why* we go through *what* we go through it becomes a recipe for frustration. Sometimes the frustration of life is so burdensome that we're tempted to curse the day we were born. Remember Job? He was an Old Testament patriarch, who understood such feelings. Amid his personal turmoil, he said to God:

> *Let the day perish wherein I was born, and the night in which it was said, there is a man child conceived.* (Job 3:3 NKJV)

Job could relate to our need to make sense out of what is seemingly nonsense. The search for understanding life's rollercoaster of events are endless and, in many cases, even unsuccessful. Like the dry, dusty throat of a thirsty man lost in a desert, we reach for so many solutions and philosophies that we suppose will quench this thirst. To our dismay, we find ourselves drinking the dust of disillusionment. Empty and discouraged, we throw up our hands in defeat and resort to merely existing in this life. Herein lies the inevitable birthing of the attitude *que sera, sera*, whatever will be, will be. In theological circles, this attitude and philosophy is known as fatalism.

For almost a decade of William's life after his divorce from his wife and resignation of his ministry from the religious denomination with whom he held ministry credentials, this was the way he saw himself. For the first time in his life he would have no denomination to cover and support his future in ministry, no family name to depend upon, and no hopes of growing old with the mother of his children and celebrating the traditional fiftieth year wedding anniversary. All he was left with in the world was his relationship and hope in God. Looking back at it all, this was exactly where God needed William in order to fulfill His purpose in his life. William never saw these unfortunate details of his life coming, but it was written.

Unfortunately, William fell prey to thinking that all his efforts didn't matter. He felt as if he was assigned to a certain fate that would disqualify him from God's original plans in ministry. Each night he prayed that such a fate would not befall him. Thinking this way is a recipe for frustration. So often, we set a course for ourselves, only to veer off toward places we never intended—or worse, come to a stand-still we can't seem to shake. Then, it's only natural to wonder if we've either missed God's best for our lives, or just never saw it clearly to begin with. I'm here to tell you that it is not too late. God hasn't given up on you. He hasn't taken your destiny and given it to someone more worthy.[1]

Here in lies the fault with the philosophy of fatalism, it does not encourage understanding, nor does it enforce the pursuit of purpose. Fatalism implies that we are all subject to life without the benefit of personal choice, life without our cooperation and the intentional pursuit of purpose.

Purpose is best known as one's destiny. To understand destiny is to embrace the fact that your life has been predetermined or predestined. Each of us has a God-given purpose. God has destiny in mind for us. Its potential echoes now and for eternity. It reconciles mankind back to its Heavenly Father. Our God-given purpose meets a God-sized need. It calls us to a destiny that God wrote on our hearts before the creation of time.[2]

When you embrace this fact, you must also embrace the fact that nothing occurs in life without reason or purpose. Without proper direction, we live our lives never knowing the purpose or reason for our experiences, whether good or bad. Knowing and understanding the reason for these experiences will ease the pressures of life and place all events, good or bad, in their proper perspective. Proper perspective may be defined as *the view in which an idea or experience fits that brings completeness, ease, and understanding.*

Perspective, therefore, must be indorsed by a legitimate source of understanding that is based on truth before it can be considered *proper.* Not every perspective is proper, especially in our search for the *why* of life. The most common mistake made by the seekers of truth and meaning is to look for the answers to the questions in life from life itself. The key to understanding life is not in life itself, but in the source of life—God. So our search should begin with understanding the source of life, for in this search, we will understand the origin and purpose of life.

Behind the curtain of "cause" everything that exists has a beginning, and since it has a beginning, then it is safe to assume that there was an intended purpose. Purpose began as an idea in the mind of God, the source. A plan for the idea was laid and then initiated. But before the idea, plan, and the purpose, there existed something much more important, the void. The void can be described as emptiness or need. In his book, *Northern Memoirs,* Richard Franck said, "Necessity is the mother of invention." Or to paraphrase, necessity gives birth to creation. Therefore, everything that is, is because of something or someone that exists, but is incomplete, invalid, or unresolved (necessity).

If we apply these statements to life, it will be clear that life can be understood only through the source of life and that if life was given, there was first a need or a void to be filled. After this, *the idea* of you came into the scheme of eternal planning as the means to which the need will be filled. This need, in turn, created the purpose for your existence. The plan of God represents the course upon which all events will take place. In essence, it is the road that you must travel that will prepare, shape, and define you for your purpose.

> When there is a lack of understanding the reason *why* we go through *what* we go through, the experience becomes a recipe for frustration.

In the beginning, it was inconceivable for William to understand how God would use the conflicts of his ministry and marriage to fulfill a higher purpose in his life. He was ostracized by his peers in ministry, restricted from preaching in denominational churches where he frequented and had annual standing invitations. He was told, and even in some cases, it was prophesied that his leaving would yield an unfruitful ministry and that his life would be cursed if he didn't return to the denominational covering. Needless to say, God knew what He had in mind for William; plans to prepare him beyond the limitations and control of a denomination and to give him a hope and an expected end that could not have been achieved where he was, at that time.

Let me take a moment at this point to share an important truth. One that I hope will free others as I have been freed in my past experiences. I have discovered in my relationship with God and through my trials in life that not all prophesy is from God and not every word spoken is anointed. I had to learn the hard way that religious people will at times confuse spiritual discernment with being carnally suspicious, and they will impose their personal convictions on others by clandestinely inserting the phrase that "God spoke to their spirit" as a precursor to their "Word from the Lord." Now, I am a firm believer in spiritual gifts, and I know that God will use individuals as messengers and vessels of impartation, utterances of correction, judgment, and blessings. My statements above are intended for those individuals who abuse spiritual gifts and who use God's name in vain for their own personal agendas. These individuals, if allowed, could hinder your pursuit of God's ultimate purpose for your life. So be careful and discerning about who you allow to speak into your life. As the Scriptures advises us:

> *Beloved, do not believe every spirit, but test the spirits to see whether they are from God, for many false prophets have gone out into the world.* (1 John 4:1 ASV)

The Pursuit of Purpose Is a Continuum

Your pursuit of purpose is a vital element to how you view your experiences. I embrace the concept that this road to fulfilling our purpose is a continuum. That through every experience (good or bad) there are many other purposes that we are fulfilling along the way. Clearly stated, I believe that while we are being prepared, shaped, and defined on this predetermined road through life's experiences such as love and relationships, we are also fulfilling intermediate purposes that lead us to our ultimate purpose in life. Our ultimate purpose is the sum total of all that we are to accomplish in life, intermediate pitfalls and poor decisions, although frustrating, are a part of the process.

Each level of maturity is determined by how well we learn from the events we encounter in life (cause and effect). Events are experiences we live out in life. They are divinely prearranged to fit a certain cause God has determined necessary for where and what He have prepared for us. It is when one understands that there is a reason for the pitfalls that the path is easier to travel. This understanding will bring ease to the frustration of the journey, an answer to the uncertainty of the unseen, and clarity to the mystery that continues to unfold in life.

Then comes our ability to accept that everything we encounter in life is simply a part of the perfecting process of life itself. It is one thing to know that it is a part of the process, yet it is another thing to accept it. We must get to the place where we accept that this process is preparation for maximum living and our effective functioning in this world. Like it or not, it is a God-truth and there is no getting around it. The sooner we discover and begin to internalize this truth, the sooner we can begin to reassess life's experiences and begin to add value and meaning to what we have gone through.

Positioning Yourself for God's Blessings and Prosperity

It was amazing to see how God would intersect William's life with the individuals that were critical for his success and for the next chapter in his life. Imagine where William would be at this point of his story if he chose to lament over his losses and accept harmful information about his future. Let us go a step further. What if William wasn't in the educational, spiritual, and physical place at the appointed time when his path crossed with Bishop Potter or Chancellor Colson? All of the opportunities that we have seen come into William life would not have been possible. It would be like God placing you in this world to be a certified public accountant so that you could impact a certain corporate environment, but you never push yourself to complete college. Then one day, when it was His appointed time to intersect your life with the person and the opportunity, you were not qualified to be considered for the position. The larger picture of William's story is that God was orchestrating every single detail to its completion, but William needed to be properly prepared and properly positioned.

Let me state it this way, William's responsibility within God plan was to prepare for his future, to listen and obey God's direction, to walk through the current open doors, to work with integrity and passion wherever God led him, and to trust God for the results and the next open door. In essence, where God was taking William was already predetermined. How he would get there existed within the parameters of God's written plan for William's life.

Personal empowerment and spiritual development is critical if we are to position ourselves for the blessing and prosperity God desires for us. Although there have been some not so Godly teachings on prosperity, I do believe in the principle of prosperity. To me, prosperity is the residual effect of the perfecting process experienced in the seasonal changes in life. I further contend that prosperity is much more than the acquisition of assets, liquid or tangible. It is a much deeper valuation of self. For this reason, assets should not be the consuming focus in your life, nor should it be an issue of constant concern; it should just *be* as a result of your earnest pursuit of knowing and fulfilling your purpose.

In Matthew 6:33, Christ declares, "But seek ye first the kingdom of God and His righteousness, and all of these things will be added unto you." Therefore, our objective in life should be to pursue that which is considered the proper perspective (that which is right in the eyes of God, our source). This will allow the prosperity that has already been predetermined and assigned to our journey in life, to be released in our lives at the time and place intended.

King Solomon wrote, "To everything there is a season, and a time to every purpose under the heaven" (Ecclesiastes 3:1). By divine authorization, this wise king was sharing with the world a principle for understanding the

> Behind the curtain of cause is purpose—it is the reason why someone is born, or why something happens.

mystery of life's eventful journey. This principle affirms that the divine plan of life consists of these two facts: (1) everything we experience in life has been assigned to specific seasons, (2) like the natural seasons of the earth, they are timed to fulfill a specific purpose on the road of destiny. In reality, nothing is by chance. Everything has a purpose. Whatever you're experiencing in life, whether negative or positive, it is for your good. Therefore, know that the season you're experiencing this very moment will not last forever; it is on a divine timer that is due to expire at the point of achieving its assigned purpose.

Another Face of Cause and Effect

At the beginning of this chapter we took a look at cause and effect in reference to the relationship between actions and events such that one or more are the result of the other or others. Simply stated, a cause is *why* something happens, and the effect is *what* happens. Behind the curtain of cause is purpose—the reason why something needs to happen.

As we close Chapter 14, we shall look at another face of cause and effect. In its generic scientific term, it is the law of attraction, which is also known in the Bible as the law of sowing and reaping. It is a universal law. Like all universal laws, the law of sowing and reaping is extremely important to grasp if you are to learn to attract the blessings and favor of God that you desire into your life.

Like all other universal laws that have been put into place by God, the law of cause and effect is unchanging, unwavering, deliberate, and precise in its application and delivery. It, like all of the other universal laws, knows no prejudice and delivers in exact proportion the same to all, regardless of belief, age, gender, origin, or religion based on the seeds that you choose to plant.

Think of your experiences as the fruit of a seed you have sown. You can trace every experience you have ever had back a one single seed of choice or decision. A seed-decision was sown in the ground of a moment in your life and in time or in its season, the fruit of that moment came into fruition. Hence the very familiar biblical principles, "Do not be deceived, God is not mocked; for whatever a man sows, that he will also reap" (Galatians 6:7 NKJV). The other says, "But this I say: He who sows sparingly will also reap sparingly, and he who sows bountifully will also reap bountifully" (2 Corinthians 9:6 NKJV). The first reference speaks to your deeds— what you put in. On the other hand, the second reference speaks to your proportion—how much you put in.

The key person of interest in this principle is YOU. What are you sowing as it relates to your future in the area of education, career, relationships, finances, and your spiritual life? How much of your self—your passion are you investing in your future aspirations? Keep in mind, whatever you put in is what you can expect to return back to you when it is time. Every choice has a consequence. If we make wise, Godly decisions, we can expect God to reward us for our consistent trust in Him and His word. If we make impulsive or corrupt choices, we can anticipate negative consequences.

Both verses describes an unalterable law that affects everyone in all areas of life—family, work, finances, and pleasure. It is both a warning and an encouragement. Unlike man made laws, it is inescapable and delivers back to you the results of whatever you give within the parameters of your life experiences and opportunities. This is dependent on whatever action or inaction you choose to take—or not take.

Our return in life is always in proportion to whatever we have given of our self. For example, the student who invest time in study

> Every choice has a ripple effect of consequences.

and preparation will get the pleasure and satisfaction of valuable knowledge which sharpens his intellectual acumen. This student cannot stay hidden behind closed doors, but rather in the world he's been chosen to make impact on, the door of life will open for him. He will never need to hold his head down in shame, but he will have the courage to face the challenges which confront us all in life. The opposite is true for the student who approaches his preparation for life with a lackadaisical attitude and a minimalist effort that pleads for passion.

A robust faith is required to comprehend and accept the purpose behind the curtain of cause. A tenacious desire to succeed is necessary to firmly grasp the principles that are critical for purpose to be fulfilled, yet we know how seldom such thoughts enter our mind. We habitually stand in our situations in life and look back by faith to see the past filled with God and His plans. We look forward and see Him inhabiting our future; but our now is uninhabited except for ourselves. This is because we fail to invite Him to participate in our affairs fearing He may not want what we desire or perhaps He may not agree with decisions we want to make.

In the eternal scheme of things, we are not so eager to search for truth—to know and see what God has in store for us behind the curtain of cause. In fact, it is not we who are pursuing after God. It is God calling after us! If it were not for God's concern for us, His desire to make known the amazing life we can have in Him, and the unfathomable purpose He has planned for us, we would be forever forsaken. God relentlessly pursues man because He knows He is our greatest need. Even though we rebel against Him and pursue our own sin-filled interests, His quest continues. *While you were doing all these things, declares the Lord, I spoke to you again and again, but you did not listen; I called you, but you did not answer* (Jeremiah 7:13 paraphrased). What an astonishing thought! Behind the curtain of cause—eternal purpose, heaven's splendor: Almighty God is in pursuit of you and me.

Chapter 15

ONCE MORE TO LOVE (STORY)

Atlanta, Georgia 2007

A WARM SUMMER NIGHT'S breeze blew through the Atlanta downtown area as William and a few other ministers exited the convention center after the last service of the evening. They had just attended an annual Empowerment Conference across the street from the Omni Hotel at the CNN Center. William was invited to join the others for a late dinner, but he was tired and seemed preoccupied. So he declined their offer, returned to his hotel room, showered, brushed his teeth, and debated about whether or not to order room service. He really didn't have much of an appetite, so he chose not to. Instead, he ate a granola bar and drank a bottle of Ocean Spray cranberry juice from his small refrigerator.

William sat at the desk, picked up the remote and turned on the television. Nothing much was on so he signed onto his laptop computer to check his emails. While waiting for his system to boot up, he leaned back in his chair, clasped his hands behind his head and began to think about all the day's events. In the midst of his replaying his day, a déjà vu moment eased into his thoughts. It occurred to William that he was in this hotel before under different circumstances. It was 1993, and he was in Atlanta for a conference hosted by a Ministerial Fellowship where he was contemplating bringing his ministry under, after resigning from his former denomination. William was at a major crossroad in his life. It was there he had an unusual experience with God, and himself. This began his journey of self-discovery. This time William's visit was more of a celebration of sorts. Fourteen years ago, his life took on new dimensions and he was in a good place in his ministry, and his life was back on the right track.

To Mother My Dearest

The trip was also a bitter-sweet time of memories. Today was June Fourteenth, his father's birthday. William lost his father January twenty-second, five months earlier, to colon cancer. Seven years earlier his lovely and beloved mother passed away from pancreatic cancer. Although William and his father mended their broken relationship and was able to have meaningful interactions and share special moments in the latter part of his father's life, his mother was the crowning jewel and the seasoned corner stone that steadied his life. She had a radiating golden brilliance, an undeniable presence that lit any room she entered. Her quiet demeanor and exquisite looks accented her soft spoken voice that could calm the most troubled spirit. She was his voice of reason, the muse that inspired William to view the world differently.

Her death was hard on William as it was for the other siblings. Her illness went undisclosed until her final few months the spring of 2000. It was on Mother's Day weekend when she was admitted to the hospital. She never came home again. For William, it was as if she lived long enough to ensure that God would keep His promise to him. For it was when he was a teenager that William experienced his unusual call to ministry, and she was the only one he trusted to make sense out of the experience.

She always knew what William was thinking and feeling—because they shared the same passion for life. She stood by him when all others doubted his resolve when everything around him collapsed. She was his pearl—his gemstone; very rare, refined, admirable, and most cherished. It is said that the first woman to love a man is his mother and that a man will love his wife best, but his mother the longest. Since her passing, her loving presence lingered with William still.

William's concentration was broken when his AOL account opened with the familiar voice notification at that time announcing, "You've got mail!" It showed several new messages. As he scrolled through the list of senders, he noticed a familiar childhood classmate, with whom he played sports, who had sent him an invitation to their thirty year high school class reunion. William was surprised to get any notifications from his classmates in Georgia, since he didn't graduate with them, but from another high school. He replied to the invitation anyway. The invitation was sent through a website called Classmates. While reviewing the invitation and the details of the class reunion, William was curious about whether or not the high school he graduated from in Jacksonville, Florida was also having a class reunion.

So he searched the website for Jean Ribault Senior High School. To his dismay, he didn't see a class reunion notification. But, he did find that the website listed the names and contact information of the students who attended the school from their sophomore year to their senior year. With his curiosity stirred, William continued searching for people he possibly knew. Line by line he scrolled, through a hundred or so names, until he came upon a familiar name of a girl he was sure he knew. Her name was Rose Elaine Lafleur. "Could it be her?" he thought. The timeline listing that she attended Ribault from 1978-1980 was accurate. It was very much possible.

William recalled a young lady he met during the summer of 1976 when he relocated to Jacksonville, Florida to finish high school. "That was over thirty years ago," he thought. Rose was the younger sister of Monique Lafleur. He met Rose at the church where her family and relatives were members. His father's church was in the same district and in the same denomination. During the months when there was a fifth Sunday, all of the churches in the district would come together for fellowship services. William was good friends with their uncle, Palmer Parrish, who introduced Monique to William.

Monique and William became friends. However, it wasn't until later that William became aware of Rose. But when he did, something very special happened inside of him. He developed a crush on Rose back then, but she was five years younger and painfully shy. So they never really talked nor did they become closely acquainted. He would see her periodically at different church functions and one particular time at their home when he visited with her uncle Palmer. He remembered her sitting across the room quiet and reserved— taking in all of what was going on around her. She was beautiful. Even then, she was unassuming and poised. There was a persona about her that reminded William of his mother. Though he hadn't seen her in three decades, seeing her name and the possibility of it actually being her, took his breath away just as it did the day he first laid eyes on her.

Fortunately for William, the Classmates website had an email address for her. He struggled with if he should send an email. William said to himself, "I wonder if this is really Monique's sister." "It has to be. After all, Lafleur is not a common African American name." he thought. So William sent her an email reintroducing himself and asking if she was the sister of Monique Lafleur. He didn't receive a reply email that night. In his mind, perhaps it would be unlikely that the email would get to her. People tend to change their email addresses often. William wondered what would have happened if they had dated when she was old enough. He often thought of her throughout his adult life. For the rest of the night William could think of nothing else except for the possibility of hearing from Rose and different events where he saw her when they were younger. He reminisced of how simple and pure things were back then—even love or at least the idea of love.

Love Lost and Found

Since going through a divorce at the worst time in his life, love was something that William stayed clear of. He focused more on finding out who he was as an adult man and minister. All of his passion had been directed in one single direction, to discover and fulfill the meaning of his life. He didn't want to entrust his heart to a relationship again. In his mind, love was too fragile and vulnerable. Love, he surmised, had the potential of causing irreparable damage to him and his ministry aspirations. It almost destroyed him the first time around. Although he dated a few times and was once involved in a close long-term relationship, he knew the demands of his ministry would always become an issue.

William was at a point in his life where he and ministry were one. He intentionally avoided falling in love. To him, love was a luxury he could no longer afford to risk his ministry for. He vowed never to get married again and to never to subject another to the demands his ministry which was brought to bear on him. By now, he was well aware that not everyone possessed the innate fortitude and sacrificial lifestyle that is paramount, the vocation of the ministry.

William's failed marriage brought him to his proverbial knees. After his marriage ended, he was to the point of going through counseling. He wanted to get an objective voice about what he was going through. He was weary of religious legalistic individuals who obviously didn't have a clue about what he was encountering at that time in his life. Instead, William made a decision that turned out to be the foundation of the next level in his ministry that God would eventually reveal to him. So, rather than to spend money on a therapist, William enrolled in graduate school to study theology and psychology with an emphasis on Christian counseling. The duel major would assist him in developing a deeper understanding God's position on the psychological, as well as, the spiritual well-being of individuals. It would allow William an opportunity to gain the proper perspective on his own life.

Love, he knew, was an awesome experience; but it also had proven to be this mysterious and powerful emotion that have defeated some individuals, complicated his own life, and seemed to have been the central source of joy and suffering for so many others. He followed his fractured fascination with love, marriage, and ministry into the halls of academia. In actuality, it was his own therapy that he sought.

As William approached the final phase of his doctorate program at Xavier Christian University, his internship involved working with couples and families. He was mesmerized by the intensity of their struggles and the way they often spoke of their relationships in terms of life and death. Twenty years after his own divorce from the mother of his children, William was amazed that he felt exhilarated when he sat down in a room to work with a couple and witnessed the moment when their partners suddenly understood one another's heartfelt messages and risked reaching out to each other. Their struggle and determination daily enlightened and inspired William to keep his own precious connection with love alive. Although, he hadn't involved himself in a relationship that could summon his love to resurface, there was always the hope of the possibility.

And Then There Was Rose

After that night in Atlanta, William returned home several days later. But still there was no reply email from Rose. He managed to keep himself busy for the next several weeks, but during that time, his curiosity grew about whether his childhood crush had received his email. If so, would she remember him? Would Rose reply or not?

One month later, when his mind had begun to erase the chance that she may reply and accepted the fact that it just wasn't meant to be, William received an email from none other than Rose Elaine Lafleur. She did remember him and was equally excited about reconnecting with an old acquaintance. In that moment, it was as if spring was there with its blossoming flowers and chirping birds just like in the movies. The only thing that was missing was the musical score. You know, that appropriate song played at the appropriate time in the background of a story complementing the unfolding scene of two lives whose paths crossed in a prior lifetime reconnecting.

William caught his breath and opened the email. Rose was cordial and kind. The tone of her writing signaled that the young girl he knew had evolved in a mature woman. She mentioned that she now lived in Maryland. Methodically, she began to recall all of the memories that were familiar to them both.

As the months passed, Rose and William continued to communicate via email. They grew closer and was forming a comfortable bond. Weekly phone calls became the norm. They shared life experiences with each other—their good times and bad times, their successes and failures. They were transparent about their failed marriages, and about the lessons they had learned in the process. William talked about his ministry, how important it was to his future going forward. He shared how the pressures and responsibilities of his ministry contributed to not only his failed marriage, but how he had approached relationships since that time; never again allowing his heart to be penetrated.

The truth was, William had begun to open himself and his heart up to Rose on a subconscious level and in a way he had never considered before. He was beginning to love again. In addition, the unusual frequency of contact and transparency was new territory for William. He never liked talking on the phone except for business. Opening himself up to love again, especially long distance, would have instinctively raise a red flag and alerted his defense mechanism to begin its rise. Still he continued on this uncharted course.

One day Rose expressed that she was planning to fly down to Jacksonville, Florida in two weeks to pick up her daughter who had spent the summer with her grandmother. William was thrilled by the news and the wheels in his mind began to turn. He thought this would be an amazing opportunity to actually come face to face with Rose. If this were possible, it would be the first time William would have seen her since she was thirteen years old. The thought of meeting Rose after all those years was overwhelming. Rose too, was excited about the possibility. So they began to make arrangements to meet.

They both, though anxious and curious, were careful and cautious of moving the relationship too fast too soon. Unknown to Rose, William had already crossed the theoretical prospect of a possible relationship. He was pacing himself in the footsteps he believed were predestined and made for him in anticipation of his life traveling on this pathway. For William, nothing was by chance. There was a reason for why he and Rose's life intersected again.

They made plans to meet very briefly in the Jacksonville International Airport. Rose shared her travel itinerary with William. They were to meet in the restaurant area of the airport for just thirty minutes prior to her and her daughter's flight. It was a perfect safe plan. They would meet in the early morning. It would be brief enough to not make more of than it was meant to be, and long enough to get reacquainted and to enjoy one another's company.

William had a meeting scheduled that same day of their meeting but later that evening back in Ft. Lauderdale. Rose thought it would be too much for William to attempt to drive back to south Florida in the same day. Little did she know, that not only was William driving back the same day, he had planned to drive up to Jacksonville the night before and come straight to the airport without sleeping over.

Two weeks seemed like two years to William, but finally it was Friday, the day before the trip to Jacksonville had come. All day long William thought of seeing Rose again. That day at his office seem to drag by. At home, William began going through a mental checklist of things he needed to take care of before he left. By bed time he couldn't sleep—he was too excited. He had been up, and moving about since about Midnight. William was scheduled to leave for Jacksonville at three o'clock that morning, but he couldn't wait.

With only an hour of sleep, William showered, dressed, secured the house, got in his car and began his trip. There were no cars in sight on the I-95 highway northbound.

He had a four hour drive ahead of him. Rose's flight was scheduled to depart at 8:00 A.M. Their meeting was at 7:00 A.M. Because William left an hour earlier than planned, he would arrive at Jacksonville International Airport at least an hour early. That would give him enough time to relax and to gather his thoughts. Not only was he meeting Rose for the first time, but he would also be meeting her daughter, Animee D.

William arrived at the airport and parked in the parking garage adjacent to the departure flight entrance. He sat there in his car with the music playing, not really listening. He was able to see from a distance cars pulling up to drop off its passengers. William thought to himself that it never occurred to him to ask Rose what type of car or what color the car would be that was driving she and her daughter to the airport. He didn't want them to beat him in the restaurant area. William wanted to already be seated and waiting on them to appear.

So, William immediately turned his car radio off and exited his car. He took the parking garage elevator one floor down to the walkway of the airport entrance. It was still dark. William was unable to see if any of the cars that were pulling into the drop off lane was Rose's ride. As he crossed the last lane of the driveway and stepped onto the sidewalk at the doorway of the entrance, a car pulled up. He slowed his stride down slightly, but not enough to draw attention. In his peripheral line of sight he caught a glimpse of a woman who favored Rose. As he cleared the concrete pillar that separated them he realized it was in fact Rose.

William wasn't sure if she saw him or not, but he hurried to the appointed meeting spot while Rose and her daughter checked their bags and saw her family members off. William moved around to several tables, attempting to find the perfect spot. But more so, he was working through his nervous energy that seemed to get worse by the second after catching a glimpse of Rose. Even though, it was just the side of her face and a shadow of her hand moving in the flashing headlight of a passing car, he felt like that same teenage boy who was introduced to this gorgeous girl, but he never got a chance to really get to know.

Fifteen minutes passed, and he wondered what had happen to Rose and her daughter. He knew he was early, perhaps it wasn't her. In the same breath William saw Rose and her daughter walking toward him. They didn't see William, so they sat several tables across from him in the atrium. William moved from the table where he was sitting and walked over toward the atrium. As he neared, Rose looked up and finally saw him. Her face lit up with a gentle innocent smile. She slightly raised her hand to wave, almost as if not wanting to bring too much attention to the moment, but just enough to acknowledge that she saw William and for William to see her.

By the time William reached the table Rose stood up. They embraced and William whispered in her ear, "Can you believe this?" Clinging to Rose for just a few seconds longer, she shook her head as her eyes fluttered with excitement. Her face seemed to pale with shyness. Then Rose broke the embrace and turned around to introduce her daughter to William. She said, "Animee, this is William, an old friend of mine and a friend of our family. We have known each other for years. Our families became acquainted through the church we attended a long time ago before you and the other kids were born." Animee cordially greeted William and began bantering as if she had always known him.

Shortly after the introduction, they got something to eat and return back to their table. The awkwardness of anticipation and awe and comfort of the first embrace was now behind them. William looked up into the face of this instantly familiar woman who resembled the teenage girl he used to know. He realized that even though they had been communicating, nothing could have prepared him for what he was feeling at that very moment.

Rose began to talk about when she was still living in Jacksonville before relocating to Maryland. William was breathless as they discussed the opportunities that could have brought their paths together years earlier. Many times before, they were in the same city, in the same area, but never running into each other. Later in the conversation they discovered that for months Rose corporate offices were located on the south side of Jacksonville only five to ten minutes from where William often stayed when he was in town on business for the university. The Embassy Suites hotel was only a few miles from her offices. They both were in disbelief.

Their thirty minutes were up. They passed so quickly. It was time for Rose and Animee to prepare to go through security and board their flight back to Maryland. William stood up and helped Rose from her seat. Animee came around and gave William a hug. William told Animee how pleased he was to meet her, and he smiled, and she said the same. William reached out and embrace Rose. Unlike the initial greeting and hug, Rose held William firmly and was not so quick to break the embrace and William responded in like manner. After a kiss on the cheek, William walked the two to their security gate. Not wanting the moment to end, he watched them clear security and continued to relocate himself not to lose sight of them until they were no longer visible.

William walked back to his car thinking about how remarkable his visit was with Rose and her daughter. Rose had evolved on so many levels since their youth. She had matured into a well-traveled, well educated, accomplished career woman, and mother. Although she had faced many challenges, some life threatening, it was clear that God had a purpose and a plan for her life because she championed each one of them and she was still here.

As William drove back to south Florida, he replayed his brief visit over and over in is mind during the drive. He memorized the contour of her face and every facial gesture she made at different points of their conversation. By the time William made it back home in Boca Raton, he was so enthralled with reconnecting with

Rose that he totally forgot the meeting he had schedule in Ft. Lauderdale that evening. It was a conference call which worked in his favor because he didn't want to unknowingly get caught blushing as random thoughts of Rose and his experience with her earlier uncontrollably entered his mind.

Later that night, as William is lying in bed just before falling off to sleep, he would always feel his mother's presence with him as he prayed. Perhaps it was his thoughts of her undying love or the visual of her sweet smiling face that William would summon at will whenever he needed to feel her near. Her presence was like a warm cloak of unseen solace that wrapped around him. At night, when the world was still and quiet, he would remember the woman who loved him first; then he drifted off to sleep.

This particular night was a very different night for William. Although he went through his ritual of praying and remembering, his mother's presence did not cloak him as usual. For a moment, he thought it was strange, but he continued to wait for the feeling he had always felt. But the feeling never came. Nevertheless, he was at peace. He felt a stillness in his spirit, and a sense that if it were possible, perhaps this was a sign that his mother was letting him know that she was no longer needed in his life in that form. Above all, that God was once again fulfilling His promise to him through another—Rose.

After being reintroduced to Rose, William's reluctance in the past toward love dwindled over time. Perhaps, God was using this unusual reconnection to resolve a part of him that was dormant for a reason beyond the obvious. Yes, love was the obvious reason. But still, there was more behind the curtain of love than what met the eye. William was sure of it. He had come to know God as the Source of the unusual. Nothing in his life ever came easy nor was the traditional his norm. There seemed to always be a deeper meaning or purpose to most of his experiences. So why would this be any different?

From the moment William met Rose, they felt an indescribable quality of closeness. Of course, they were not completely clueless concerning love's potential of pulling the shades of disillusionment over the eyes of the enamored. They both understood that nobody was perfect and that if they were to consider a life together, they would have their own unique set of issues to contend with. On several occasions, William and Rose expressed that they weren't expecting perfection so much as the intense connection. For William, he needed it to feel a divine connection as well.

William felt the intense connection with Rose at the initial meeting in Jacksonville where he felt that heady first-blush excitement that launched his comeback to love. But, it wasn't until his mother's presence lifted, that he felt that the divine connection was confirmed. As far as William was concerned, he had found his soul-mate and life partner. Two years passed, and as it was meant to be, William and Rose were married. Love pulled him in, even though in times past, he pushed it away.

William's life had been inundated with challenges, redefined by trials, and cultivated through transitions. Looking back, his life somewhat mirrored that of the Old Testament trial of Job who lost everything—children, property and wealth, good name, his health, and his wife. In the end, the adversary of life was silenced. Job's suspicious friends were silenced. But God was not. The God of *how* spoke and restored Job's good fortune. William's life, in the end, like Job, surpassed his beginning, "And the Lord turned the captivity of Job, when he prayed for his friends: also the Lord gave Job twice as much as he had before." (Job 42:10 KJV)

Rebirth, reconciliation, and restoration were the common threads that wove through the tapestry of William's life story; but his personal struggles with affirmation and lost love could also be seen. In the end, William experienced life changing triumph in all the areas of his life. It did not come fast or easy, but it was well worth the bout and the wait.

Erica Jong, an American author and teacher best known for her fiction and poetry, had this to say about life and love, "It really is worth fighting for, being brave for, risking everything for. And the trouble is, if you don't risk anything, your risk is even greater." William couldn't agree more because he decided to risk everything to rediscover his life and his ability to love.

Chapter 16

LIFE FULL CIRCLE

Strategically Organized Experiences

USUALLY, WHEN IT IS said that something or someone has come full circle after going through some experiences and changes, they are now the same place as they were at the beginning. This was not so for William. William's life had come full circle, but he was certainly not at the same place he began. He was in a much better place. Certainly, God did restore everything that was affected during his decade of turbulence. Even more, He restored everything to William, but on a very different level. So perhaps it would be fitting to say that he had come full circle and then some.

The collection of short stories on the life of William were arranged strategically to reflect the cycles of growth in his life. They display how he strived, failed, and tried again through varies challenges. The stories reflect a man forever seeking to make sense of his ministry and life as it continued to unfold. Throughout the process, William desired to develop a better understanding concerning the awful moments, as well as, the extraordinary moments in life. The experiences that leave the unexplained moments lingering and hints of a thread which, if we were to pull it, might utterly unravel and redefine who we are and who we are becoming.

In the book of Job, during his suffering, Job must have sought for answers to the same mysteries of life as William. After all, why would God allow such

> God interrupts moments of blessings and contentment in our life with a season of tests and trials for a higher purpose.

tragedy when you are doing everything you know how to please him? The writings of Sigmund Freud and C. S. Lewis help us to understand the nature of such a question. Often we have difficulty seeing the purpose behind God allowing suffering, namely, our tendency to distort our image of God.

In his book, *The Question of God: C.S. Lewis and Sigmund Freud Debate God, Love, Sex, and the Meaning of Life*, author Dr. Armand M. Nicholi, Jr. showcases the debate of these two diametrically opposed points of view. Freud (an unbeliever) and Lewis (an atheist turned believer) both came to the same conclusion about Ultimate Authority. Nicholi writes:

> "If we possess a strong tendency to displace or transfer feelings from parental authority, especially the father, onto present-day authority figures, how much more might we distort our concept of an Ultimate Authority whom we cannot experience with our senses? If this holds true, we must be careful that our concept of God—whether the God we reject as unbelievers or that we worship as believers—is firmly based on the Creator revealed in history and not our neurotic distortion of Him."[1]

This same distortion about God being the Ultimate Authority still boggles the mind of mankind. We struggle with His decisions that unfold on earth in our lives. This is evident in the book of Job.

As a result, a key question arises when we evaluate the events in the book of Job, "Can a favored, righteous person hold on to his faith in God when things go wrong?" In a conversation with Satan, God argues that such a person can indeed persevere, and points out his servant Job as an example. God then allows Satan to visit terrible trials upon Job to test him. To Job, his life was unraveling right before his eyes.

Could it be then that God interrupts moments of blessings and contentment in our life with a season of tests and trials for a higher purpose? According to the story of Job, this is exactly what He did. If this is so, then we must also concede that all experiences are strategically organized for God's divine purpose. These experiences cannot always be understood in human terms. Because of that, we tend to take experiences we don't understand very personally, even to the point of questioning God's intentions.

Job's indignation toward God was obvious. He said:

> *If I sin, what did I do to you, you watcher of humanity? Why have you made me your target?* (Job 7:20 paraphrased)

This is the exact response most of us have when we are confronted with unpleasant circumstances and issues that we feel are unwarranted. Our feelings are ignited with anger and heightened even more when others view our misfortune as an issue with our faith, or our commitment to God. Make no mistake; there are some issues in life that do merit corrective measures by God. Yet, in Job's case there were no obvious issues directing God's decision to allow these experiences in his life.

Three of Job's friends responded to his troubles in the identical manner as some in our circle of friends may respond. Job's friends, including Elihu, said that God distributes outcomes to each person as his or her actions deserve. As a result of this belief, they insist that Job has committed some wrongdoing to merit his punishment.

This view of God and how He interacts with us through experiences is obviously flawed. When you look at the circle of life experiences and the mystery behind God's sovereignty, you should know not to attempt to dispense divine justice based on human rationale. God's power and purpose is so great that humans cannot possibly justify His ways. His ways are beyond our finite understanding.

God blast Job for attempting to explain His intentions or His reason for what He does or does not do, "Have you comprehended the breadth of the earth? Tell me, if you know all this" (38:18 NKJV). In essence, God challenges Job to explain the details of His creation—to tell God how He framed the world. Even though He responds to Job, God himself declines to present a rational explanation for the seemingly unfair distribution of blessings among men. Now, I know each one of us have posed and pondered the question of why some experiences seem unfair or why blessings are given to the undeserving. When the rubber meets the road and life comes full circle, we discover that it is not about God's actions toward us or even us versus others, but rather, what is God's purpose in the circle of experiences visited upon us?

After reading the book Job, we get a clear understanding about how to view our own experiences in life. We, like Job, are full of questions and concerns about why bad things happen to good people and good things seem to come to the bad. We unknowingly, are questioning God's plans and purpose in this world. I am glad that God did not need to respond to us the way he did to Job. God's onslaught of rhetorical questions to Job, asking if Job can perform the same things He can do, overwhelms both Job and the reader of the book of Job with the sense of God's all-encompassing wisdom, awesome power, and unfathomable plans.

Circles in the Cycle of Life

Circles of experiences lie within the cycles or seasons of life. In my previous book, *Necessary Changes*, I invited the readers to embark on a healing journey through the four cyclical seasons that we all must experience to reshape our "thought life" for maximum living. King Solomon, in the book of Ecclesiastes, gives us some insight on what I call "Circles in the Cycle of Life." He writes:

> *There is a time for everything, and a season for every activity under heaven.* (3:1 NIV)

He continues in the next verses to confirm that God does chose to allow certain experiences to take place at certain times in our life. King Solomon list a few normal human cycles of activities we can relate to which are: life, work, physical, emotional, relational, diplomacy, politics, and even military. All of these activities go through a cycle or season, and within each cycle lies circles of experiences that must come full circle for the purpose of bringing us to a full understanding of the purpose for each experience.

But King Solomon doesn't leave us hanging with just the knowledge of circles within a cycle (season). He further confirms God's participation and general purpose in human affairs by saying:

> *I have seen the burden God has laid on men. He has made everything beautiful in its time.* (Ecclesiastes 3: 10-11 NIV)

In essence, do not sweat the bad stuff in life! God has not only allowed the burden you're experiencing, but He has orchestrated its outcome. Not only are you going to be alright, when you come full circle in this experience, God's intention is to make you beautiful, to glorify you in the presence of your critics. In return, you are expected to transfer the glory back to Him. The transfer of glory is necessary so that the world will know that *God is* and that *He is a rewarder of those who diligently seek Him.*

So often in life we go the full circle. We wander off the right path this way or that way, even for years. But, one way or another we find ourselves coming back to where we started from, or somewhere symbolically similar. We fall into an unhealthy pattern of doing the same things over and over again expecting different results. Sometimes, we attribute those circle of experiences as coming full circle in life only to reap the fruit of dissatisfaction. According to King Solomon's disclosure of God's seasons, when you come full circle you should be a better person in a better place.

> Don't sweat the bad stuff! God not only allowed it, He has also orchestrated its outcome in your favor.

Life presents both major and minor circles of experiences for us to walk and live in. From the day we arrive on the earth and cuddled in our mother's arms, there is more to see and more to experience than can ever be seen or experienced. There is more to do than can ever be done. Throughout the entire Bible, we can see that the whole intention behind the life circles is to allow us to experience our own personal growth and expansion. In the major and minor process of our growth, we find that we are being groomed to become qualified vessels of influence in the earth. Our intended role then is to impact others, and influence them on behalf of God and His Kingdom purpose.

A New Level of Mastery

Coming full circle in life should reflect a new level of mastery. Personal mastery means you are committed to lifestyle improvement on a continual basis. Mastery is the driving force behind successful individuals. It is the ultimate goal in everything they do. Life is a circular ongoing journey of learning as we go through issues and cyclical processes. This is why things that are theoretically new often seem very familiar. It is also why, whenever we work to release a tradition, change a pattern, or overcome a fear, we often come face to face with that issue one last time before we get to the point of true break-through, even after we thought we had conquered it. However, if we can hold on to our determination through one last test, we will realize a new level of mastery in our lives.

Mastery also implies that because you value your personal gifts and talents, you set up structures and support in your life in order to fully and reliably express them. Mastery does not prevent the unfolding of these gifts and talents, but catalyzes and sustains them. If you find that you are losing momentum in your pursuits in life, and that you are not making any forward movement in life, this is an indication that you have not come full circle and have not reached the level of mastery. A closer look at the details of your experience is necessary. A determination of what God is saying to you through the experience is needed.

The personal growth and expansion in the circle of life involve processing us through internal struggles, weaknesses, underlying proclivities, and egos. At birth we are as a precious and unconscious bundle of love and potential. From that moment on, we absorb, respond to and learn from the many influences around us. Watching and mirroring our parents and guardians, we gradually perceive ourselves as individuals separate from others. We adopt beliefs, opinions, preferences, characteristics and habits. Our personhood continues to take shape as we are exposed to the world outside of our home and parents.

When the influence of our parents integrates with the influences of the outside world, it often creates conflicting aspects of our personality and our perspective, especially, if our home influence was built

> Becoming who you were meant to be means living above daily distractions and ungodly influences—it means living life at a level of mastery.

on a biblical foundation. Slowly, we grow with internal struggles and evolve physically, emotionally, mentally, and spiritually with what borders on warfare. The circles in the cycle of life is intended to create internal synergy between your desires and God's intentions.

Your innate gifts and talents creates the desires and dream that you have. They are God-given. However, until you submit them to God, they are continuously being influenced by the persuasions of the world, pushing farther away from what really belongs to you. When internal synergy is achieved through the circles in the cycle of life, it bridges that gap between your desires and God's intention for your life. Your personal life grows, your spiritual life strengthens, and you place God in the driver's seat to your destiny. Submitting to Him, includes assuming complete responsibility for following His directions in your life.

In doing so, God obligates Himself to bring you into the knowledge of the things you need to know, and also into the company of the people you need to know that is critical for your success and destiny in life. Becoming who you are meant to be means living above the person you would be if you gave in to the distractions of the ungodly influences we all face in this world. The power to become who you were meant to be comes from listening to the stirring of the soul when God speaks. It is then you will be in harmony with God, and you will know that the unfolding of your life and your potential of your success can not be made to happen from the level of ego nor from worldly motivation. It can only happen when you are where you are supposed to be and when God determines and creates the right conditions.

A Divine Difference

When we come full circle, because we have weathered the storms of life, we experience a wholeness of sorts. We come out somehow different. We should, because at the very least, we know with God's direction and care, we handled the challenges we were faced with that seemed insurmountable when we began our journey. We feel empowered and courageous that we took on the burden of change and succeeded in the process. Having conquered this particular cycle to its full term, it warrants a moment of pause and reflection before we move on to the next challenge that life will unreservedly present to us.

As we take a final look at the end of Job's saga (Chapters 40-42), we see God finally interrupts Job's complaints, calling from a whirlwind and demanding Job to be brave and respond to his questions. God's questions are rhetorical, intending to show just how little Job knows about creation and how much power God alone has. God describes many detailed aspects of his creation, praising especially his creation of two large beasts, the Behemoth and Leviathan. These were enormously large land and sea creatures whose exact identity is unknown.

> *Behold, Behemoth, which I made as I made you; he eats grass like an ox. Behold, his strength in his loins, and his power in the muscles of his belly. He makes his tail stiff like a cedar; the sinews of his thighs are knit together. His bones are tubes of bronze, his limbs like bars of iron. He is the first of the works of God; let him who made him bring near his sword!* (Job 40:15-19 ESV)

And,

> *Can you draw out Leviathan with a fishhook or press down his tongue with a cord? Can you put a rope in his nose or pierce his jaw with a hook? Will he make many pleas to you? Will he speak to you soft words? Will he make a covenant with you to take him for your servant forever? Will you play with him as with a bird, or will you put him on a leash for your girls? Will traders bargain over him?*
>
> *Will they divide him up among the merchants? Can you fill his skin with harpoons or his head with fishing*

spears? Lay your hands on him; remember the battle—
you will not do it again! (Job 41:1-8 ESV)

Overwhelmed by the encounter, Job acknowledges God's unlimited power and admits the limitations of his human knowledge. This response pleases God, but He is upset with Eliphaz, Bildad, and Zophar for spouting poor and theologically unsound advice. Job intercedes on their behalf, and God forgives them. God returns Job's health, providing him with twice as much property and wealth as before, new children, and an extremely long life.

There was a distinct divine and personal different in Job once his life came full circle in that experience cycle. What made Job different is exactly what should make us different once we too have been tested, we shall come forth as gold (Job 23:10). Gold implies being better, of more value, and solid through and through. It represents change both internal and external. It stems from a change in mindset and branches out from there. In truth, we are constantly moving toward some things, and away from others. But in order for noticeable transformation to occur, we must pass through a series of seasons (circles in a life cycle) in succession.

This does not mean that a personal change can't take place quickly, because it can. What it does mean is that all meaningful change, regardless of the time required, will follow a certain sequence—circles in the cycle of life (seasons).

The Mountaintop Perspective

As we conclude the topic of life coming full circle, there is one last thought I'd like to leave with you. Life coming full circle is like stepping onto a mountaintop where after wandering in the wilderness below, for a moment, we have the vantage point of altitude. We can see where we came from, and where we are standing at the same time. It is important to remember that we will be tested again. Yet, we should pause and take a look at the path we have traveled; honor God and how He navigated us through our circle of experiences. We should celebrate our persistence, and embrace the good success we can now enjoy because of our obedience to His will. Then we can begin the next chapter of our circular journey with a fuller understanding of where we are coming from. It will serve as a memorial to our faith in where we are going and in our God who will determine how we will get there.

God can do his work through you, even when you don't understand how. To obtain the "big picture direction" concerning where God wants you to flow, it will take reflection, prayer, and honest feedback from others. God is not trying to keep secrets from you. Ask Him to give you "big-picture direction" for your future, and to guide you in making daily choices. The One who called you faithful, and He will do it.[2]

For a man to conquer himself
is the first and noblest of all
Victories.
~ Plato

Chapter 17

TRIUMPHS: GOD'S ULTIMATE PURPOSE BEHIND TRIALS AND TRANSITIONS

TRIUMPHANT LIVING IS ONE of the characteristics that God wants to develop in us by the work of His grace. Even when we are in difficult situations, the Lord wants us to learn to walk in the victory that is available to us in Christ. Through the trials and the transitions in life, Christ leads us into triumph; we do not accomplish this ourselves. This triumph is a spiritual victory that belongs to us by being in Christ. *Thanks be to God who always leads us in triumph in Christ* (2 Corinthians 2:14). Our victory is not spasmodic but continuous. The Lord "always" causes us to triumph; every time in every battle! We are not *up* today, and *down* tomorrow.

Triumphs are the God-certainties of success and deliverance that is predetermined in heaven before they are released in the earth. Triumph over *self* and then over life is paramount and the proper divine order of purpose. Whether over *self* or life, triumphs are first acknowledged by you, and secondly they are recognized by the world because they represent the improbable outcomes to you or your known unbearable circumstances. Triumphs are your opportunities to transfer glory to the God of *how*. Transferred glory points the world to the all-powerful, all-knowing, and ever-present God.

When a person is triumphant, it means that they are successful—they are winners. Whatever battles they are faced with, they are the victors. Triumphant individuals champion their challenges, and conquer the crisis they have been chosen to process through to its God-ordained end. As Christians we must understand that triumphs involve spiritual warfare, and both are defensive and aggressive. Never before in the history of the Church have the assaults upon Christians been more learned, more persistent, more malignant than in the last decade. Satan has launched his attacks on the body of Christ without apology or excuse.

Since the beginning of Christianity, Satan's agenda has been to take out anyone who represents the Kingdom of God. He takes it very personally. We as believers in Christ and as ministers of the new covenant are captives of Christ—He took captive those taken captive by Satan and now we are His captives (2 Cor. 2:14)! Here the Greek verb for *took* means leading men as captives in a triumphal procession. Christ is a victorious General: He defeated Satan, and He took his captive to be Christ's! Now we all, as believers in Christ, need to allow Christ daily to defeat us and subdue us so that we may follow Him as the General in His triumphal procession to scatter the fragrance of Christ everywhere!

Satan is not thrilled about our newfound triumphal fragrance. He attacks us whenever and wherever he thinks it hurts. He pushes the buttons of vulnerability and wait for us to crumble in self-defeat. His desire is to spoil the fragrance of victory. For this reason, triumph must be defensive and aggressive.

Triumphs are Defensive

Triumphs are defensive because they protect your God ordained destiny to be triumphant. Triumphs' success are based on divine tactics and adaptation to God's historically proven principles, plans, and procedures critical for your steady growth. Satan gives his unholy spiritual army their marching orders with strategic plans to confront every individual in this world—believers and unbelievers alike. His objective is simple: to deceive and to destroy lives. He achieves this by causing confusion, delusions, misdirection, and attempting to defuse God-given dreams.

> When a person is triumphant, it means they are successful—it means they are winners in the arena of life.

This truth exist in the mere fact that we all fight battles everyday of our lives. These battles may be in our minds with doubts, fears, anger or bitterness; or they may be physical battles with sickness and disease. The battles may be with a sour relationship with one's spouse or parents or children or boss or pastor or neighbor. The battles may be with the pressure of lack of money to pay bills or the temptation to go after quick prosperity through illegal or unethical means. Because we are human, these battles we all face rips us up and tears us apart.

But the God of *how* gave us His Son, Jesus Christ, for us to win in life. He gave us His Son for our freedom, not only from the penalty of sin which is death, but also for an abundant lifestyle. He now lives in us as the *hope of glory* and has given us the promise that *greater is He who is in us than he who is in the world*. Yes, these are wonderful promises to know, but applying them in everyday life is certainly far more difficult than simply memorizing the verse.

John wrote these amazing verses in his first epistle. In 1 John 5:4, 5 it says:

> *For whatever is born of God **overcomes** the world. And this is the **victory** that has **overcome** the world—our faith. Who is he who **overcomes** the world, but he who believes that Jesus is the Son of God.*

That is why we sing songs like, *Victory in Jesus.* The Greek word for victory is *nike* which means conquest or victory. The word for overcome is *nikeo* which is the verb form of *nike.* Conquest, victory, and triumph are synonymous. Throughout the Scriptures, the Old and New Testament, God has given us the defensive means to triumph. His divine tactics involve historically proven principles, plans, and procedures to overcome our spiritual enemies.

Many Christians do not realize they are adamantly resisting any surrender of the power and effects of bad memories or events that hinder their lives. They replay their inner tapes of anger and guilt over bad memories, failures and humiliations over and over never stopping. As I have stated in previous chapters, your past's only function is to be the part of your life you have learned from and overcome. It is your reference point to show the magnitude of what God has done for you so you can show others what He will do for them.

Triumph is God's defense of who He is. Triumph is the release of negative things in your life. It is God's manifested deliverance of negative influences of the world from your destiny. Triumph guards your mental processes. When triumph shows up, it crushes and smashes the deceptions of the enemy trying to confuse you.

We wrestle, or strive and struggle in our minds against world systems, the flesh or the carnal nature, and the devil. The mind involves our thoughts (imagination, reasoning, and intellect), as well as our emotions and will. In all of these aspects lie the very heart of an individual. By our thoughts and feelings we make certain determinations and develop our will. It is with the mind that we either surrender or resist the purpose of God for our lives. Author Vance Havner once said:

> "We cannot change our hearts, but we can change our minds; and when we change our minds, then God will change our hearts."

The triumphant Christian knows that the renewed mind is the *how* of changing your heart. The next step in renewing the mind is to put into operation the Word of God which you have placed in your heart. Do it! Live it! You must realize that renewing the mind is your responsibility and not an involuntary action done for you by God. Yet, while understanding your responsibility is essential, it is not intended to be done with the exclusion of God.

As Christians, we should seek to live by the truth and power of God because they are our assurance of God's promised triumphs in each and every situation in life. We are not ignorant of the reality of ungodly influences, and the deception that surrounds our world on a daily basis. It is in this process that we will encounter a very real spiritual struggle in our thoughts, emotions and will. This is conceivable because the adversary knows that these areas are directly related to the power of our faith, and means to receiving the promises of God. The adversary's primary goal is to weaken the faith of every Christian.

Triumphs are Aggressive

Triumphs are aggressive (offensive) because they require an all-out effort on your part to win or succeed. God has obligated Himself to us to ensure our triumphant outcome if we do our part. Nothing you attempt for God should be done with a haphazard half-hearted effort. We must understand God's strategy for being *more than conquers through Christ Jesus* (Romans 8:37) and we must be aggressive in our faith. The "more than conquerors" are those whose faith wins in the mind before the actual confrontation takes place.

James Allen had this to say about the mind:

> "A man's mind may be likened to a garden, which may be intelligently cultivated or allowed to run wild; but whether cultivated or neglected, it must, and will, bring forth. If no useful seeds are put into

it, then an abundance of useless weed seeds will fall
therein, and will continue to produce their kind."

The useless weed seeds James Allen refer to will produce what
the Bible call "strongholds." Most minds come into the state of
salvation stubbornly filled with old attitudes, wrong patterns of
thinking and some pretty strange ideas. Many of these old ideas
and attitudes will be protected by self-erected strongholds. Their
concepts of God are usually formed from old ideas rather than
the truth.

But God has provided the principles, plans, and procedures for
properly and aggressively conquering these strongholds that snuff-
out dreams and destroy lives. He has given us spiritual keys and
weapons to facilitate our triumphant aggression. Second Corinthians
10:4-5 (KJV) tells us:

> *...the weapons of our warfare are not carnal, but
> mighty through God to the pulling down of strongholds.
> Casting down imaginations, and every high thing
> that exalteth itself against the knowledge of God, and
> bringing into captivity every thought to the obedience
> of Christ.*

Aggressive faith produces triumph by trusting the God of *how* and His word to tear down and destroy the sources of personal strongholds such as: bad attitudes, negative patterns of thinking, questionable ideas, sinful desires, tainted beliefs, bad habits, behaviors learned from ungodly sources, generational bondages and wrong words spoken about us, to us, and by us—just to name a few.

> Triumph is God's defense of who He is to the world. It is His gift to you for transcending destructive influences and circumstances in your life.

Strongholds are deceptions that have taken hold in a person's mind. It's an incorrect thinking pattern based on a believed lie. People can get incorrect perceptions of God by listening to Satan as he tells them how God doesn't love them, etc. People can feel like dirty old sinners when they believe Satan's accusations as he continually reminds them of their past (which has been washed away!). Strongholds are based on lies from the devil. They can come in the form of deception or accusations. Accusations always lead to guilt and the feeling of unworthiness, which weighs you down and tears you apart spiritually.

Since strongholds are built upon lies that we have been fed, the way we tear down strongholds is by feeding on the truth (in God's Word), which is the opposite of what the enemy has been feeding us. If the enemy has been feeding us a lie, we need to stop eating the lie and start feeding ourselves the truth.

Triumphs are Driven and Directed by Wisdom

One book in the New Testament offers wisdom to help God's people live a triumphant life. The Holy Spirit, through James—the Lord's half-brother, gave us principles of wisdom and instructions for dealing with testing and trials, for developing Godly wisdom, for strengthening our belief in the goodness of God, for increasing our faith, and for knowing the importance of our words. In all of these things, James never lets us forget that Jesus is our example of triumphant living.

Wisdom is another critical aspect of triumph. Wisdom is the ability to discern accurately and to know how to deal prudently with people or circumstances. This kind of discernment does not come from the mind, but from the spirit. However, it might be said that wisdom is knowledge in action—the successful use of accumulated spiritual knowledge.

Wisdom will direct our thoughts, control our tongues, guide our steps, and protect our ways. There are three Greek words used in the New Testament which are all translated "wisdom." *Sunesis* is the kind of wisdom relating to understanding and intelligence; *phronesis* is practical wisdom, what we might call good old common sense; and *Sophos* is the ability to discern what is happening in a situation and to look ahead, with hope, to a good end. *Sophos* wisdom "sees through" what is happening and inspires patience.[1]

Triumphs Require Proper Uniform and Weaponry

In every case, trials involve a warfare that demand we tap into our spiritual resources: wisdom for the strategy of God, the proper uniform and weaponry for an aggressive defensive and offensive attacks. They are critical to our being triumphant. The enemy seeks to rob us of strength in spirit, soul, and body. With aggressive faith, we encounter trials like a soldier going forth into battle! Never forget that God has equipped us to be soldiers from head to toe:

> *Finally, be strong in the Lord and in the strength of his might. 11. Put on the whole armor of God, that you may be able to stand against the schemes of the devil. 12. For we do not wrestle against flesh and blood, but against the rulers, against the authorities, against the cosmic powers over this present darkness, against the spiritual forces of evil in the heavenly places. 13. Therefore take up the whole armor of God, that you may be able to withstand in the evil day, and having done all, to stand firm. 14. Stand therefore, having fastened on the belt of truth, and shaving put on the breastplate of righteousness, 15. and, as shoes for your feet, having put on the readiness given by the gospel of peace. 16. In all circumstances take up the shield of faith, with which you can extinguish all the flaming darts of the evil one; 17. and take the helmet of salvation, and the sword of the Spirit, which is the*

> word of God, 18. praying at all times in the Spirit,
> with all prayer and supplication. (Ephesians 6:10-18
> ESV)[2]

We have the ultimate fire power. Nothing and no one can withstand the arsenal of God. He has promised us in His word, *No weapon formed against you shall prosper...* (Isaiah 54:17). Such a promise, when taken to heart, will make you fearless—a force to be reckoned with. When your vision fills up with the greatness of God, you become fearless. You go about whatever it is God has given you to do. Don't flatter Satan's pride by showing interest in his limited and temporary power, but look at the greatness of Jesus Christ. The Bible says the God of peace will crush Satan under your feet (Romans 16:20), that God has prepared an everlasting fire for him and his demons (Matthew 25:41). That rabid dog will no longer continue to menace the children of God—it is going to be put down. So whatever it is that God has given you to do in life, go about it knowing that you can be protected, you can be prayerful, and you can be fearless and triumphant.

Triumphs Thrive on the Presence and Glory of God

> Strongholds are deceptions that have subdued your mine. They are incorrect thinking patterns based on a believed lie.

If we want to attract a consistent flow of triumph in our life, then we must abide in the presence and the glory of the almighty God. We must constantly practice the presence of God to stand against these trials as victors. To be overcomers, we must also stay full of the Word of God through daily reading and meditation. Above all, we need to seek the Lord in prayer when we find ourselves surrounded by crisis. We need His presence around and within us to access the fullness of triumphant living.

The principle for practicing His presence through His word and through prayer and meditation is the secret of all successful living. Making God a part of our very consciousness, something which Paul describes as *praying without ceasing.* (1 Thessalonians 5:17)

Unfortunately, many Christians don't live as though God dwells with them. The rest of creation seems to be doing what they were created to do. "The heavens declare the glory of God; the skies proclaim the work of His hands" (Psalms 19:1). The animal kingdom reflects the glory of God: the migratory birds know when to fly south for the winter; squirrels store up for the winter; bears hibernate. All living creatures operated by divine instinct, but they are not created in the image of God as is mankind.

If we are to be triumphant, why is it that we often struggle to live as God's temple? The place where His presence is obvious to the world around us. We were never designed by God to operate independently of Him. When we become the dwelling place of God, and function by the power of the Holy Spirit, then we glorify God. Like all of God's creation, as we triumph in life, we should instinctively (naturally) live to transfer the glory from our life of conquest to God. After all, triumph, in the end, is God's intended results in our life after we have successfully processed through trials and transitions.

Epilogue

IN RETROSPECT—THIS BOOK
(MY TESTIMONY)

Temple Hills, Maryland

WRITING *THE GOD OF How* has been an extreme pleasure and labor of love. In writing this book, I wanted to keep my perspectives straight and do justice to both the personal stories and the biblical and psychological principles—the conceptual and the experiential. Toward that end, I clustered theological truth and slices of my life story into different chapters and moved back and forth between these perspectives and transitions. I believe that from such binocular vision, the Word of God becomes a living and breathing manual for His Kingdom in the earth as it is in heaven.

As I neared bringing this manuscript to its end, I thought it would be robbery not to share my most recent testimony with you, the reader. It was the inspiration needed to give birth to the critical elements of this book. It is amazing what you can accomplish when you are forced to take time from life's busy schedule. There are insights and the inspirational nuggets of wisdom that avail themselves to you when you're alone with God. They are unplanned solitary moments thrust upon you—a time commanding your undivided attention leaving you with no other choice but to sit and listen to the Divine One.

On November 27, 2012, while on my way to work, I was involved in an automobile accident that literally changed the course of my life. I'd stopped at a red signal light off of Route 5, exiting onto Allentown Road. I was in the right lane of a double lane road that turned left onto Allentown Road. Next to me in the left lane was a mid-size car. Once the signal light turned green, I proceeded to make my turn. The lady in the car next to me seemed to be preoccupied and sped up without following the left turn flow of traffic. It was as if she was attempting to drive straight across the highway instead of making the prescribed turn along with the rest of us turning onto Allentown Road.

Upon colliding with my vehicle, the other car pushed my vehicle across the double-lane major highway. The sound of squealing tires and the smell of burning rubber as they rubbed against the bent frame of my rear fender while sliding sideways, and the scrapping of metal from the other car as it was forcefully peeling my rear panel apart, was silenced as my car finally rested against the concrete median of the entrance ramp on the opposite side of Allentown Road.

Amazingly, the accident seemed minor because neither of us appeared to have any injuries. We called the police department, who informed us that since both cars were drivable and there were no apparent injuries, all we needed to do was exchange insurance and license information. The lady vehemently apologized, and she immediately called her insurance company admitting fault. I contacted my insurance company as well. They informed me to drive it directly to the nearest BMW collision center. I ensured that the lady was okay, and we went our separate ways.

Several days after the accident, I began experiencing neck pain and stiffness in my lower back. I assumed the pain was just bruised muscles or minor trauma which is to be expected from the type of impact my car experienced, but I still did not feel a trip to the emergency room was necessary.

After a week of constant pain, my wife, Kathy suggested that I go to a chiropractor as a precaution and at the very least, get some physical therapy to address the pain I was experiencing. After researching a few websites, we made a selection from a list of practitioners, and we scheduled an appointment. My initial visit yielded two x-rays and three sessions of physical therapy. During my last session with the chiropractor, he recommended that I have an MRI done because he noticed that three of my upper cervical disc were fractured and I may require surgery.

Again, Kathy and I began looking for a specialist in the area of orthopedic surgery. We were referred to an amazing surgeon in Washington, D.C. He ordered x-rays and an MRI. The results of the tests revealed something far more critical than just three fractured disc. According to my orthopedic specialist, the fractured disc were the least of my concerns. His diagnosis was that I had severe spinal stenosis. There was an acute narrowing of the spinal canal because of degenerative changes in my bone structure and disc. I was informed that had this condition not been discovered, within a year, I would have been totally paralyzed from my neck down for the rest of my life. My doctor informed me that I needed surgery as soon as possible. At that moment, my life took an abrupt turn, of course, into totally unchartered waters.

I was forced to make immediate modifications in my life, postponing travel plans, assigning substitutes for the coming semesters, and canceling a host of speaking engagements. Life as I knew it had come to a screeching halt. Several months later, April 10, 2013, I went in for surgery to correct this condition. While in surgery, they found massive bone growth behind my cervical disc which did not show up on the MRI. The condition was worse than diagnosed. A one hour surgical procedure turned into three and a half hours. The surgeon reported that he had to remove a significant amount of bone growth from the cervical spine that could have punctured the spinal cord if not corrected, and it would have cause total paralysis.

Several spinal disc were removed and prepared for bone grafts to be packed into metal cages secured by screws, and an elongated metal plate. Needless to say, I was in excruciating pain. Because the surgery required a three inch incision across my neck, and for my esophagus and voice box to be moved, I lost my voice for several weeks, I was immobilized and restricted to the first floor of our home. I was in a full hard neck-brace 24/7, even while sleeping. I was on a liquid diet for several weeks because the surgery involved manipulating my esophagus. My convalescent period extended from April through July of 2013. Like anyone experiencing such a life altering chain of events, I questioned, why did this happen –at this point in my life? I never could have fathom that a minor auto accident and surgery would have cause such a pause in my life. Even now, at the penning of this manuscript, I am still in recovery and rehabilitation.

But here is the miracle behind my recent trial and transition—it was the *how* of God's purpose that was revealed. God knew that Satan wanted to end, or at the very least, restrict my ministry by using a degenerative spinal condition to paralyze me for the rest of my life. But God, in His infinite wisdom, used an unforeseen automobile accident to uncover what was lurking beyond what the physical eyes could see and beyond what the initial X-ray would reflect.

Yes, my BMW was damaged! Yes, I was in pain and needed physical therapy! Yes, I would be inconvenienced financially, physically, and professionally! But God! He knew that there was a deeper plan and purpose in my pain. He knew that there was a book that needed to be written, and He used my convalescence to slow me down long enough to write it. This was definitely one of those unplanned solitary moments that I mentioned at the beginning of this epilogue where God commands your undivided attention leaving you with no other choice but to sit and listen to Him.

He knew that, in the end, my trial and transition would serve as a testimony to others who can't understand why God would allow bad things to happen to good people. Not only that, but also to understand that even tragedies are preordained, planned, and orchestrated for our benefit and for His ultimate glory.

Perhaps you are going through something right now in your life, or maybe you know someone who is on the brink of throwing in the towel and giving up on life. This book was written just for you. It was inspired to bring healing and understanding to life's most challenging and darkest moments. Always remember, things may look dark and bleak for a moment, but they can change. With the night and day, God has given us creation's visual of hope. No matter what happens, the sun always rises. You have every reason to believe for a miracle. I did. You have every right to believe that God will never abandon you. King David, the psalmist, and his son King Solomon wrote the following two affirmations from God's perspective and from their experiences with Him.

David wrote:

> *His favor is for life; Weeping may endure for a night, but joy comes in the morning.* (Psalms 30:5)

And Solomon expresses that,

> *The end of a matter is better than its beginning.* (Ecclesiastes 7:8)

Whether you are experiencing a day, night, or season in your life, it doesn't matter how things look in the midst of it. According to the God of *how*, the most important thing that matters is how it ends—and everything you learn in between.

Bonus Chapter

A man's mind stretched by a new idea
Can never go back to its original dimension.
~ Oliver Wendell Holmes

BECAUSE I CONSIDER THIS book to be the sequel to my last book *Necessary Changes,* I would like to include excerpts from Chapter 13 entitled *The Warm Embrace of Spring: A Time of New Possibilities.*

Excerpt: Necessary Changes (Chapter 13)

One morning I was awakened by the sound of my next-door neighbor mowing his lawn. The sunlight pierced through the slightly closed blinds of my bedroom window. Slowly, I got out of bed and walked over to the window. As I opened the blinds, the brilliant beams of sunlight scanned over my entire body. The warmth was like the embrace of my mother's loving arms. The yard was filled with a flourishing new coat of green, comprising thousands of blades of grass and hundreds of fresh blossoms. The trees and the flowers stretched forth their branches and stems toward the sky as if they, too, were being drawn into the arms of their loving Creator. He touched the womb of their fruitful existence with His arms of life. He spoke prosperity and growth into their seasonal process. The moment was filled with an ambiance of new possibilities, and I was there.

> Make decisions with a new sense of purpose and with the clarity of a renewed mind.

I'd always anticipated the spring season. For me, it was a time of new beginnings. Observing nature's blooming beauty seemed to impose its possibilities in my life. In many ways, it represented survival, more so, preservation while going through the refining fire of life. I have carried you on a journey with me through the seasons of refinement. If you're like me, whom I'm still in my state of becoming, you will concur with me that it has been, and still is, an eye-opening experience.

We've made it through the trial heat of summer, the cool pruning of fall, and the cold refinement of winter. Now we enter into the season that many await with baited breath, the season of spring. Nothing captures the true essence of the anticipation of new possibilities like the ambiance that accompanies the season of spring. Spring is definitely a time for blissful thinking. During this season, your mind will be open to clarity, creativity, and courageous and purposeful dreaming. You will no longer see yourself and the world through the previous tunnel vision. The dreamer in you that has longed to come forth can now take their rightful place in this world!

It is similar to the budding of a tree or the blooming of flowers at springtime. The ambiance is right ... the environment has been prepared, and the vegetation of the earth cooperates with their destiny (God's timing to come forth and produce their fruit). So if you have come through the seasonal changes, the ambiance is conducive, and the ground of your life is prepared for you to walk in line with or step into destiny and fulfill your purpose in life. Your potential gifts and talents are ready to emerge to assist you; all that is now needed is your awareness to the results of your renovated life. Take time to identify what changes have taken place in your thinking, your response to different situations, and how you coordinate your daily life as a whole. Now is the time to pay close attention to the details of your life. Because you are now planted in fertile soil, prosperity and divine promise will be yours. The burden of hopelessness has been replaced with success and personal fulfillment.

The bottom line is that you're starting a fresh. You are now presented with a new lease on life. Embrace it with all of your heart, soul, and spirit. Be careful not to instinctively backstroke into old patterns and methods of operations. Check yourself daily and intentionally. Make every decision with a new sense of purpose and clarity of thought based on your renewed mind. At first it may be mentally taxing, but eventually it will be like breathing air involuntarily, and you won't have to think twice about making decisions in the realm of truth. You have a built-in mechanism that will alert you to any possible problems or issues. The Spirit of God that dwells in you will guide you. During your seasons of refinement, you opened up your life to His direction and empowerment, so allow Him to advise you step-by-step for the remainder of your life's journey.

This is not about *spiritual spookyism*. I'm referring to the innate impressions upon your heart, your mind, and your soul that can only come from the divine. You will unmistakably identify with what is a God idea, that is, the counsel of the infinite mind, versus your *old man* nature impulse. Because you are a refined person of purpose, anything that is not in line with truth will bring pause in your life and conflict in your heart. The choice, though obvious, will still be yours to make. Now that you have been cautioned, let's delve into some important aspects of your new beginning.

Take Time to Identify What Changes Have Taken Place in Your Thinking

A question came to mind as I prepared to write Chapter 13 regarding the warm embrace of spring. The ambiance of possibilities is potent and all around you, but the question that is always asked and must be answered is: How do I bring these possibilities into my life or within my realm? You may ask whether this question has merit. Think with me for a moment. Has there been a time when you were in an environment with others who were elated and celebrating, but you could not connect with the excitement? Have you ever been in a setting that was ignited in celebration and noticed someone who looked like they didn't belong or seemed to have been on a date with the "Grinch Who Stole Christmas"? Well, that same scenario applies here. Possibilities are all around us, but there are some individuals who just can't get into the groove or into the flow. They fail to understand how to function in the season of possibilities.

Possibilities are attracted in the lives of individuals who possess and function in what I call the spirit of B.E.T. No, it is not the acronym for Black Entertainment Television. This one stands for *B*elief, *E*nthusiasm, *T*ake action. Anyone attempting to flow in spring's realm of possibilities is required to possess a personal belief that one is a candidate for possibilities. In other words, do not exempt yourself from anything God says is possible in your life. Move forward with an unshakeable spirit of expectation. Instead of dreading life, you should now embrace it. Your tears have been bottled up and have fermented throughout the passing seasons of life. In retrospect, you will drink from that vase of fermented affliction, for what was once a source of hurt is now transformed into wisdom and healing for your soul. Time processed your experience and brought illumination. Illumination exposed the lies of past failures and unlocked your possibilities. God, in His timing, has made everything beautiful and fruitful in your life. Concerning time, lies, and possibilities, William Shakespeare said, "Time's glory is to calm contending kings, to unmask falsehood, and bring truth to light." Your spring season is the fulfillment of that time in your life.

No more slow dancing to the blues of hopeless moments. You're now dancing the dance of freedom and singing the song of, "There is now no condemnation." Old things have passed away, and new things are on the horizon. I draw wisdom from Alfred Lord Tennyson who said, "The old order changeth, yielding place to the new … and God fulfills Himself in many ways, lest one good custom should corrupt the world." You are to recognize your new place in life. Actualize your new freedom by embracing and pursuing your new possibilities with everything that is within you. You may stumble on the theory of worldly common sense when pursuing the possibilities of your destiny. A main deterrent to success in life is when someone says, "Use your common sense." This advice has the potential to halt your forward movement about something you passionately want to accomplish; some persons inject that to have you rethink your plans and/or actions according to old perceptions, which were probably shaped by them.

Check Yourself Daily and Intentionally

The old maxim "Use your common sense," has its place if properly cultivated. I believe, however, that wisdom based on truth is more appropriate. Common sense is predicated on varied personal philosophies and depends on the *place* and *time* of its conception. Common sense, then, has the probability of being outdated and demographically irrelevant. Personally, I agree with Albert Einstein, a German-born theoretical physicist and the originator of the theory of relativity. He said, "Common sense is nothing more than a deposit of prejudices laid down in the mind before you reach eighteen." These are powerful words from one of the world's most esteemed individuals of his time.

Personal belief is an invaluable quality afforded to us as developing human beings. If not careful, it can be enslaved by the prejudices of common sense. The preconceived convictions and unfavorable conviction of others can be detrimental or injurious to a person who is hooked on the notion of common sense. Through focused personal belief, destiny will develop your sense of rationale; there will be nothing common about that experience. I believe that makes us all unique.

Belief

You must believe that you're a candidate for the realm of possibilities to engage your life. When the realm of possibility is engaged, we cross over the threshold of unbelief and enter into the realm of possibilities, where all things assigned to our destiny are possible, and the only limitations are those we place on ourselves. One of the most difficult concepts for many individuals to embrace is that their lives were decreed before they were even a passionate thought in their parents' minds. Your personal belief must begin with pondering this thought, "If God allowed my conception and birthing, then I am a part of His divine decree." He spoke these words to confirm this truth in the life of Jeremiah, whose name means, "Whom Jehovah has appointed." The divine decree revealed, "Before I formed you in the womb I knew you, before you were born I set you apart [decreed you]" (Jeremiah 1:5a NIV). Your possibilities are built in the divine decree of your life in the sphere of God's timing.

> Personal belief is an invaluable quality afforded to us as developing human beings.

Your personal belief will be further strengthened when you understand the meaning of decree. Decree, by theological definition, is God's plan by means of which He has determined all things that relate to the universe, including His own actions toward it and everything that comes to pass in it and of it. Therefore, by divine decree you have your existence because God determined a need for you in the world. In essence, you're here because of a void God saw in the earth that He determined only you could fill. So by divine decree, your purpose in life is predetermined, thus making it necessary for God to equip you with the potential to harness the possibilities that are already established and built into your purpose. So the season of spring in your life should be one of transcending limitations and moving into what I call the *possible impossibilities*. Therefore, I say to you, whatever truth you've discovered about the why of your existence … it *is* attainable, and whatever the plan is for you in fulfilling your destiny … it *is* possible!

Enthusiasm

An essential component of walking in the realm of springtime possibilities is enthusiasm. One definition for the word *enthusiasm* is the excited and passionate interest in, or eagerness to do something. It is an engrossing interest, something that arouses a consuming interest. Your springtime should be the object of your consuming interest. The many facets of your life that have been refined through the fires of summer; the pruned, separated, or detached debilitating issues dealt with in the fall of your life; and the purifying, meditative season of winter should have sparked a passion for new possibilities. We're born with a natural enthusiasm that can be eroded over time if we don't nourish and cultivate the seed. Like belief, enthusiasm is a quality that begins inside of us. It must be built into the full framework of the hope of those things that are made privy to us, those things that are at our grasp and are possible.

I remember well, in my late teens, how I perceived my future through the eyes of the dreamer inside me. There were so many plans, ideas, and goals I pondered each night before going to bed. They were the very thoughts I woke up to each morning that made living an anticipated and hopeful event. I had the whole world before me. In my heart and mind, I actually felt like there was nothing beyond my grasp. The span of time between my teens and early twenties seemed like one long spring season. Life was promising, and the success of my future seemed so tangible that I could almost touch and taste it. Then … I grew up!

My world was turned upside down, and the possibilities of my youth walked away from my youthful enthusiasm and fell into the adult, level-one, "think like everyone else" pessimism. As the years ensued, I began to notice that indeed, misery really does love company. I also discovered that the reason why I was being peer pressured, or should I say, subjected to friendships that obligated me into an emotional stupor, was because my enthusiasm toward life was shedding light on the uncertainties, misery, and mediocrity of many I trusted and thought were mutual dream sharers.

My challenge at hand was to find a way to recapture my God-given enthusiasm. It was a gift that I allowed others to steal away from me. The process, I later found out, was exactly what we've just come through in the reading of this text. Once I made it through the deprogramming stages and began renewing my thought-life, I experienced the resurrection of my youthful enthusiasms. Once again, the possibilities of my life reemerged. Since then, I've neither looked back nor *listened* back! The impairing voices of my past no longer had any effect on my enthusiasm. This is where you need to be at this point in your life, a proper mind-set renovated through the seasonal adjustments. This God-given gift of enthusiasm belongs to you as well. It is a treasure that should not be hidden but exposed. It should never be extinguished, but experienced; and this experience should be shared with everyone whose life intersects yours.

Your life should now be taking the shape of destiny's unique pattern, a pattern meticulously planned and purposed specifically to fit you. Use your enthusiasm to fuel movement toward your purpose. By virtue of its definition, enthusiasm is an eagerness to do something. I see enthusiasm built in a statement made by a self-made merchant, John Wanamaker, who said, "A man is not doing much until the cause he works for possesses all there is of him." Enthusiasm, when nurtured, is desire. Desire, when harnessed, is power.

Failure to nurture enthusiasm and harness desire, and failure to act on what your destiny requires you to accomplish or become, paves the way to mediocrity. The attitude of enthusiasm does make a difference. Professor Erwin H. Schell, a much-respected authority on leadership, says, "Obviously, there is something more than facilities and competence that makes for accomplishment. I have come to believe that this linkage factor, this catalyst, if you will, can be defined in a single word—*attitude*. When our attitude is right, our abilities reach a maximum of effectiveness, and good results inevitably follow." Develop your attitude of enthusiasm, for when you do, you will experience a deep, burning desire that will make your commitment to purpose a love affair with destiny.

Take Action

Your love affair with destiny will not allow you to be idle and watch life pass you by. It will stir up something within you that will require you to act upon your reason for life. Our latent abilities need a stimulant to release the potential that is stored up within. That stimulant is responsibility. You have a responsibility on your shoulders to initiate the plan for your life's purpose. You are the only one responsible for the fulfillment of your destiny. You now have to take that step of faith into the arena of life reserved especially for your participation. You've been given access to the treasures of destiny concerning why you are and who you are. The Bible states that, "To whom much is given, much is required" (Luke 12:48). Are you willing to pay the price?

Responsibility is a fair price to pay for the new possibilities that have availed themselves to you as a result of your taking action and taking charge of your life. According to our twenty-sixth president of the United States, Theodore Roosevelt, "Your ability needs responsibility to expose its possibilities." By extension, he said, "Do what you can with what you have where you are." What a profound and stimulating statement. So how does responsibility tie in with taking action? Responsibility is not only a rhetorical and theoretical position; it denotes the ability to *respond* to life's situations and tap into its reserved possibilities.

I use the term "reserved" because there is untapped potential and unlimited possibilities reserved for you. These will not be exposed or made available to you until something happens to trigger your awareness of their existence. Case in point: I was a youth, fourteen years old, thinking of the next adventure to explore in my young life. In our front yard, there was a wooden fence my father built; it was the entrance to our yard. Directly in front of the wooden fence, there stood a beautiful, tall tree with many branches extending from it. Springtime had settled in, and the acorns that adorned this tree were already visible. The lowest branch was about twice my height at that time. I'd been contemplating trying to jump the height necessary to reach the branch so that I could climb up into the tree and survey the neighborhood. I had never done it before, and the few guys in the neighborhood who had attempted it previously were unsuccessful, so I gave up the hope of ever accomplishing my goal of climbing that tree.

One day I was riding my bike around the block, which was a daily ritual. Something was about to occur that would change my perception and my life. At top speed, I approached our neighbor's house, which was located directly behind ours. The reason for this is that they had a dog named Trixie. Now Trixie, I believed, was mixed German shepherd and Fox terrier. She was an intimidating animal to be reckoned with. As long as I was on my bike at top speed, I was fine. I kind of got a kick from outrunning her on my bike; the experience made me a young champion of sorts. Well this particular day, according to my riding ritual, I built up my speed as I approached the challenging perimeter of my neighbor's yard. Like clockwork, Trixie was waiting and soon took off behind me. Normally, the chase would only last a fourth of a block and then Trixie would give up and return home. This day would prove to be different.

Our Latent Abilities Need a Stimulant to Release the Potential That Is Stored Up Within

As I approached Trixie's "give up" distance, something happened that had never happened before: my chain broke! My peddling capabilities were incapacitated (to say the least). By now, Trixie's instincts alerted her that this was a once-in-a-lifetime opportunity to make up for all her past defeats. By this time, my heart was racing, my head was throbbing, and fear quickly overshadowed me as I had already envisioned Trixie biting me, sending shock waves of pain throughout my entire body. Operating in sheer survival mode, I threw my bike on the ground and began running around the corner of the block where our house was located. I could feel Trixie's warm breath around my ankles. Her barking, mixed with an antagonizing growl, heightened my need to avoid getting caught and devoured.

As soon as I approached my front yard, my first impulse was to climb the fence, but I knew if I did, because Trixie was so close behind me, she would conquer me. Without thinking or rationalizing the challenge, I jumped straight up, and I felt

> Your ability needs responsibility to expose its possibilities—responsibility, therefore, is the fair price of realizing your true potential.

my fingers wrap around the branch of the tree I had long wanted to climb, and I pulled myself up into the tree. Unaware of what I had achieved, I sat on the branch of that tree with my arms wrapped tightly around its trunk. Needless to say, I was in sheer horror. I reluctantly glanced down to assess my situation only to witness Trixie leaping back and forth in anger … barking and growling because of her missed opportunity.

A few minutes passed, and a defeated Trixie settled down and returned home. It was at that moment that I realized what I had unknowingly and unintentionally done. The challenge that presented itself in my situation proved to be what was needed to expose my hidden potential and nurture my future possibilities of achieving whatever is in my destiny. Trixie placed the responsibility of escaping peril on my abilities, which in turn exposed my potential. In essence, you've got to take action to move and flow in the new possibilities the spring season of your life has presented. Even if it means taking one step at a time, act, attempt, and move toward the changes you want in your life, or the hope you've dreamed about. The method for transitioning from the old you to your renewed perception of yourself, and the creative ideas that now fill your fertile mind toward action, can be summed up in one of the most effective slogans I've seen in commercial advertising. In the Nike footwear commercial, these three words drive home a valuable concept: "Just do it!"

Rest in the arms of spring's warm embrace; enjoy the ambiance of the new possibilities available to you now. Don't spend time worrying about weaknesses and shortcomings. God is still working on those variables in your life; you're a *being* in process. So never use weaknesses and shortcomings as an excuse for the stagnation in your life. As you move forward, you will work through your weaknesses and shortcomings. Remember, you're evolving into the "who" you're to be; it will take a lifetime. Resolve to be proactive; don't wait until conditions are perfect, as they never will be. You should expect difficulties and obstacles as you move toward your destiny; resolve them as they arise, but make sure you keep moving. You will discover that as you keep moving toward your destiny, you will overcome one obstacle after another. Eventually, because you take action constantly in the face of life's many challenges, fear will transition from a stagnating hindrance, to a fuel—propelling you toward achieving your purpose.

Finally, begin to think in terms of *now. Tomorrow, next week, later,* and similar words often are synonymous with the failure word "never." In the words of the late president John F. Kennedy, "Never put off till tomorrow what you can do today." Take action now, dig in, and move forward toward your new possibilities. "Just do it!"

About the Author

DR. PRESTON WILLIAMS II is a prolific author, motivational speaker, and visiting professor of theology for several colleges and seminaries in the Georgia and Florida. He has held Senior Management positions with corporations such as American Express Co., IBM, and WIZA Radio Station.

He has served in Christian ministry for over 30 years. He has served as evangelist, church planter, radio talk show host and producer of "Soul2Soul" broadcast, television broadcast host of Christian broadcast "Celebrate." Under the Church of God denomination he served in the following position: District Evangelism and Home Missions Director, District Youth and Christian Education Director, Associate Pastor, and Senior Pastor.

Dr. Williams currently serves as Senior Pastor of Gateway Church, Ft. Lauderdale, Florida. He also serves Senior Vice President and recently elected as Chairman of the Board of Regents of Logos University headquartered in Jacksonville, Florida. He is a distinguished member of the Association of Christian Counselors and is a certified behavioral therapist.

Dr. Williams has worked extensively with inner-city rehabilitation centers and youth facilities providing counseling, personal guidance and leadership in at-risk communities. He has traveled nationally and internationally as a keynote speaker and seminar facilitator. He has published several books include *By the Way* (inspirational), *The Seasons of Destiny's Perfection* (personal empowerment), *Whispering Silhouette* (poetry), and *Necessary Changes* (personal empowerment).

Preston Williams II has studied at Howard University (Washington, D.C.), Lee University (Cleveland, TN), and Logos University (Jacksonville, FL) and holds a Bachelor of Arts Degree in Theology, a Master of Arts Degree in Theology & Psychology (summa cum lade), a Doctorate of Philosophy in Psychology & Christian Counseling (summa cum lade), and a Doctorate of Sacred Literature (honorary). His desire is to promote Christian education on every level and to continue his pursuit to empower lives for Kingdom purpose and productivity.

His hobbies are writing, reading, swimming, jet-skiing, and basketball. He and his wife Kathy are committed to the ministry of education and personal empowerment. They are the proud parents of five children, Preston III, Portia, Jarell, Sharmayne, and Zaynah.

Endnotes

Chapter 2

1. Philip Yancey, *Where Is God When It Hurts* (Grand Rapids, Michigan: Zondervan Publishing House, 1990), 47.
2. Ibid., 169
3. Dr. Mark D. Hanby, *Perceiving the Wheel of God* (Shippensburg, PA: Destiny Image Publishing, Inc., 1994), vii
4. Ibid., 18-19
5. Ibid., 93
6. Kay Arthur, *As Silver Refined* (Colorado Springs, Colorado: WaterBrook Press, 1997), 234-235

Chapter 4

1. Eric Fellman, *The Power Behind Positive Thinking: Unlocking Your Spiritual Potential* (New York, NY: HarperCollins Publishers, 1995), 36.
2. Ibid., 100
3. William Hines, *Leaving Yesterday Behind: A Victim No More* (Ross-shire, Great Britain: Christian Focus Publications, 1997), 137.

4. Dr. Timothy Clinton, *Turn Your Life Around: Break Free from Your Past to a New and Better You* (New York, NY: Faith Words Publisher, 2006), 133-134.

Chapter 6
1. Frank B. Minirth and Paul D. Meier, *Counseling and the Nature of Man* (Grand Rapids, Michigan: Bethany Book House, 1982), 10-11.
2. Donna Partow, *Becoming a Vessel God Can Use* (Minneapolis, Minnesota: Bethany House Publishers, 1996), 88-89.
3. Frank B. Minirth and Paul D. Meier, *Counseling and the Nature of Man* (Grand Rapids, Michigan: Bethany Book House, 1982), 10-11.

Chapter 8
1. Craig Nakken, *The Addictive Personality* (Center City, Minnesota: Hazelden Foundation, 1996), 1-2.

Chapter 10
1. H. Newton Malony, *The Psychology of Religion for Ministry* (Mahwaw, New Jersey: Paulist Press, 1995), 21.
2. Erik H. Erikson, *Identity and the Life Cycle: Selected Papers* (New York, NY: International Universities Press, 1959).
3. Mark R. McMinn, *Psychology, Theology, and Spirituality in Christian Counseling* (Wheaton, Illinois: Tyndale House Publishing, 1996), 40.
4. Ibid, 42.
5. Scott M. Peck, *People of the Lie* (New York, NY: Simon and Schuster, 1983), 252.

Chapter 12
1. Nilas Luhmann, "Familiarity, Confidence, Trust: Problems and Alternatives," *Trust: Making and Breaking Cooperative*

Relations, electronic edition, Department of Sociology, University of Oxford, Chapter 6, pp. 95.

2. Michael I, Norton, Jeana H. Frost, and Dan Ariely, "Less is more: The lure of ambiguity, or why familiarity breeds contempt," *Journal of Personality and Social Psychology* 92.1 (2007): 97.

3. Martin Gargiulo and Gokhan Ertug, "9 The dark side of trust1," *Handbook of trust research (2006)*: 165.

Chapter 14

1. Dan Erickson, *Finding Your Greater Yes: Living a Life That Echoes in Eternity* (Nashville, Tennessee: Thomas Nelson, 2006), 4.

2. Ibid., 12

Chapter 16

1. Armand M. Nicholi, Jr., *The Question of God: C.S. Lewis and Sigmund Freud Debate God, Love, Sex, and the Meaning of Life* (New York, NY: Free Press, 2002), 243.

2. Donna Partow, *Becoming a Vessel God Can Use* (Minneapolis, Minnesota: Bethany House Publishers, 1996), 193.

Chapter 17

1. W.E. Vine, *The Exhaustive Concordance of the New Testament Words* (Old Tappan: Fleming H. Revell, 1940), Vol. IV, p. 221.

2. *The Word Study Bible* (Tulsa, Oklahoma: Harrison House, Inc., 1990), 1193-1194.

Bibliography

1. Arthur, Kay. *As Silver Refined*. Colorado Springs, Colorado: WaterBrook Press, 1997.

2. Clinton, Timothy. *Turn Your Life Around: Break Free from Your Past to a New and Better You*. New York, NY: Faith Words Publisher, 2006.

3. Erickson, Dan. *Finding Your Greater Yes: Living a Life That Echoes in Eternity*. Nashville, Tennessee: Thomas Nelson, 2006.

4. Erikson, Erik H. *Identity and the Life Cycle: Selected Papers*. New York, NY: International Universities Press, 1959.

5. Fellman, Eric. *The Power Behind Positive Thinking: Unlocking Your Spiritual Potential*. New York, NY: HarperCollins Publishers, 1995.

6. Gargiulo, Martin and Gokhan Ertug. "9 The dark side of trust1." *Handbook of trust research*, 2006.

7. Hanby, Mark D. *Perceiving the Wheel of God*. Shippensburg, PA: Destiny Image Publishing, Inc., 1994.

8. Hines, William. *Leaving Yesterday Behind: A Victim No More*. Ross-shire, Great Britain: Christian Focus Publications, 1997.

9. Luhmann, Nilas. "Familiarity, Confidence, Trust: Problems and Alternatives," *Trust: Making and Breaking Cooperative Relations*, electronic edition, Department of Sociology, University of Oxford.

10. Malony, H. Newton. *The Psychology of Religion for Ministry.* Mahwaw, New Jersey: Paulist Press, 1995.

11. McMinn, Mark R. *Psychology, Theology, and Spirituality in Christian Counseling.* Wheaton, Illinois: Tyndale House Publishing, 1996.

12. Minirth, Frank B. and Paul D. Meier. *Counseling and the Nature of Man.* Grand Rapids, Michigan: Bethany Book House, 1982.

13. Nakken, Craig. *The Addictive Personality.* Center City, Minnesota: Hazelden Foundation, 1996.

14. Nicholi, Jr., Armand M. *The Question of God: C.S. Lewis and Sigmund Freud Debate God, Love, Sex, and the Meaning of Life.* New York, NY: Free Press, 2002.

15. Norton, Michael I, Jeana H. Frost, and Dan Ariely. "Less is more: The lure of ambiguity, or why familiarity breeds contempt." *Journal of Personality and Social Psychology.* 2007.

16. Partow, Donna. *Becoming a Vessel God Can Use.* Minneapolis, Minnesota: Bethany House Publishers, 1996.

17. Peck, Scott M. *People of the Lie.* New York, NY: Simon and Schuster, 1983.

18. Vine, W.E. The Exhaustive Concordance of the New Testament Words. Old Tappan: Fleming H. Revell, 1940.

19. Word Study Bible. Tulsa, Oklahoma: Harrison House, Inc., 1990.

20. Yancey, Philip. *Where Is God When It Hurts?* Grand Rapids, Michigan: Zondervan Publishing House, 1990.

By the same author:

By the Way
A Snapshot Diagnosis of the Inner-city Dilemma.

By The Way takes us beyond the theoretical and hypothetical
to the hands-on and feet-on-the-street knowledge of inner-city.
Few have written as pointedly on the subject of the inner city
and its need for true renewal through a confrontation with
the Gospel and the power of the Holy Spirit to change lives,
homes, communities, and then cities regions that are at risk.

Whispering Silhouette
The Diary of a Reluctant Poet Giving a Voice to His
Thoughts on Life, Love, and Relationships

The poetry of *Whispering Silhouette* involves not only
examining life, but also taking an honest look at the
delicate matrix of love. It was not written to be a manual
of truth, it is a poetic book of experiences, observations,
and random personal thoughts that make-up the life
of the author over a period of twenty-seven years.

Necessary Changes
A Guide through the Four Seasons of Life

Necessary Changes is about personal and spiritual life
management. It is a manual of understanding why you are
going through what you're going through at this time in
your life. It is about your relationship with yourself, your
friends, your loved ones, and the choices you must make
at different points during your journey toward becoming

the best you there can be. It is about changing those things in your life that can be changed and accepting those you cannot change, and trusting God with everything.

For further information on speaking engagements, seminars, current U.S. itinerary, and to buy copies of this book in bulk, please contact:

Preston Williams II Ministries, Inc.
(A non-profit organization)

Website: www.pw2m.org
Email: drpwii@live.com

Index